C000003214

Hi Tony

All the best with the new venture.

Regards Simon.

PASSING THE BUCK?

How to Avoid the
Third Generation
Wealth Trap

Simon is a family office consultant, educator, psychotherapist and organisational psychologist. He works with family offices and family businesses to help multi-generational families with the organisational, relational and personal aspects of their lives. From both personal and professional experience, Simon understands the complex nature of family offices and the challenges facing the different generations within them.

Simon originally trained as a teacher and rabbi, before his MSc in Organisational Psychology and qualification as an accredited psychotherapist. He is studying for his PhD in Neuroscience at King's College London and divides his time between the UK, Europe, the USA and Israel, working with individual clients, family offices, governmental and non-governmental organisations and charities. Alongside this, he is CEO of Reflections Therapy Services: bespoke individual, group and family psychotherapy clinics which are based in London and Manchester.

http://www.simonbloom-consultancy.com/

PASSING THE BUCK?

How to Avoid the Third Generation Wealth Trap

*Looking after both your wealth
and your family into the
next generations*

SIMON BLOOM

THE CHOIR PRESS

Copyright © 2015 Simon Bloom

All rights reserved. No part of this publication may be reproduced or transmitted in any form or by any means, electronic or mechanical including photocopying, recording or any information storage or retrieval system, without prior permission in writing from the publishers.

The right of Simon Bloom to be identified as the author of this work has been asserted by him in accordance with the Copyright, Designs and Patents Act 1988

First published in the United Kingdom in 2016 by

The Choir Press

ISBN 978-1-910864-35-7

Contents

Contents

Acknowledgements

I would like to thank my parents for their love and support through-out my life.

I would also like to thank my wonderful wife, Zahava, for all her unfailing support and encouragement throughout our life together, and, of course, my three children who teach me every day how hard it is to be a parent and ensure that I keep learning.

Thanks also go to Dr Rhiannon Thomas for her help working with me to compile the material from all the lectures, workshops, seminars and presentations I have given over the past few years and put it together in one place.

Introduction

Money is about value and about opportunity. And this book is about building awesome relationships, amazing lives, fantastic personalities and skills – and having exceptional experiences.

The idea of the three-generation wealth trap is one which is ingrained in our culture. The notion that the first generation makes it, the second generation merely preserves and the third generation loses it is one which has achieved almost legendary status. In this book we argue that it is not inevitable and that there are clear reasons for why it happens, along with effective ways to prevent it.

This book is for families who are worried about the apparently inevitable three-generation wealth trap and who want to learn how to have the amazing life that they deserve – and to ensure that future generations have the same. We look at the experience of life with extreme wealth from the perspectives of all three generations (with the understanding that what applies for the third generation also applies to the fourth and fifth etc.). We look at how to make sure that you truly thrive rather than just survive, and this book is not just about explaining why the three-generation wealth trap happens (although we do that clearly!) but about setting out strategies and practical solutions to avoid it.

The links between neurological science, psychology and behaviour which we describe in this book are intended as overviews of a field of research which is still (relatively) new, compared to older and more established schools of organisational and personal psychology. However, whilst the principles behind the approach to solving the three-generation wealth trap as explained in this book are very much rooted in the evolving field of neuropsychological sciences, this is not intended as an academic reference or textbook – but instead for the interested layman. For those readers who are interested to learn more about the research and science behind the theories, we have included references at the end of each chapter, but even these are only a glimpse into this exciting new area of knowledge.

In providing this glimpse, what there is not space for here is all of the debates surrounding the research findings and where research may take us all from this point. However, we wanted to emphasise that this book is rooted in neuropsychological science whilst at the same time understanding that as the field of research develops, our theories and approach will evolve accordingly. Therefore, what is presented here is, of course, an incomplete picture, but one which we hope will inform and provide an insight into this developing field and how it is revolutionising approaches to the psychology of individuals, relationships and organisations.

This book avoids stereotypes and looks, instead, at why the 'rags to riches to rags in three generations' myth is so prevalent. We do this by starting from a place which does not criticise or blame any of the generations of families for their difficulties in overcoming the challenges they face. Because that is how we see it: these are challenges which require a certain and specific set of skills, experience, abilities and understandings.

What runs throughout this book is the concept of a developmental model – of neurology, social interactions, money management, personal psychology and behaviour. By calling it 'developmental', we are emphasising the importance of seeing the challenges we face as being steps towards our goals. Whilst is it sometimes possible to take those steps at a quicker pace, what we have learned is impossible is 'skipping' too many steps without consequences in one's development towards being a healthy, well-balanced, emotionally and psychologically mature, relationally secure individual.

What this book also emphasises is that these developmental skills, experiences, abilities and understandings are different for each generation, rooted in our own neurological structures, and so it is no good to generalise. We define 'skill' as a set of repeatable and learned behaviour patterns which come from optimal brain development, based in awareness and understanding, through which we are able to achieve a certain goal or set of goals. This is different from a behavioural tendency which is engrained or develops in a natural state but is often not 'taught'.

The third generation of any ultra-wealthy family often comes in for the most extreme criticism (and, in the case of higher-profile families, that criticism is often levelled at them by the media and society in general, rather than just their peers or families). You do not have to look too hard to find a story being published about a younger member of a high-profile family behaving badly. But how fair is this and why does it seem to happen?

To use the analogy of learning to drive, the majority of the population learn on a fairly basic car with limited power. The top speed in these cars is for the most part, despite the best efforts of many new drivers, not likely to exceed their ability to control it. But what if, on the day they pass their test, they are given a supercar? At this point, very few individuals would have the skills necessary to be able to handle or manage what they have been given – with often disastrous consequences.

So it is with extreme wealth that, in effect, the third generation of a family is given a supercar before they have even passed their test. They are in possession of something which requires skill, experience and a highly developed set of abilities to be able to use it in a way which is life-enhancing rather than potentially destructive. A similar phenomenon is often seen with what are termed 'child stars' or those who are in possession of significant wealth and few of the more 'normal' limits put in place for young people. The education, social life, opportunities and aspects of life to which they are exposed are often fundamentally different from many of their contemporaries, and 'child stars' are probably the closest cousins of many third-generation individuals from ultra-wealthy families. Here we need to look even less far for numerous examples of young people who struggled to cope with their apparently blessed life. As you move from regular wealth to extreme wealth, unless you have maturity, experience, skills, ability and understanding, you will be caught out.

But as we show in this book, these struggles are unsurprising due to the fact that the wealth and opportunities do not automatically come with the experience, understanding, skills and psychological development necessary to handle them. It is of course possible to be a Jodie Foster (Yale graduate and successful adult actress), a Shirley Temple (United States ambassador and UNESCO representative) or a Ron Howard (company chairman, director, producer and devoted family man): those who have not just survived the vicissitudes of child stardom but actually thrived and gone on to build incredibly successful lives as an adult – but we are sure you can list more who have struggled and many who have not survived.

Ultimately, what this book is about is what social, psychological and organisational influences cause the three-generation wealth trap and, crucially, how intervention can prevent it. The aim is that you, your children and your grandchildren can understand better the challenges facing each of the generations (both your own and the others) and learn how to put in place effective strategies both to prevent the trap and to ensure that all the generations of the family, both those who currently exist and those who are yet to be born, live a rewarding, happy and fulfilled life where opportunities are seized and used fully. At the same time, it is important to realise that this is a process which requires commitment and, whilst the trap is avoidable, it takes significant thought and planning, rather than lip service.

It is important to be aware of the pitfalls and dangers and to understand how many challenges and difficulties wealth can bring, but there is nothing more important than love and relationships. And a family office is essentially about relationships – parents, children, grandparents, spouses, siblings, nieces and nephews.

This book starts by looking at what we call 'the root of the problem', thinking more about what we have started to think about here, looking at the underlying issues which cause so many of the problems for family offices and for the long-term stability of the financial and personal lives of wealthy families. We then, in chapters 2, 3 and 4, consider the questions which so often arise around wealth transfer and the issue of 'ownership', pointing out that the earlier generations of the family often unintentionally 'set up' future generations to fail both due to their own high-achieving personalities and due to the fact that the systems which are in place are inadvertently creating structures which gradually deplete the family of ambition, motivation and drive – all things which were crucial for the successes of the first generation. As with this entire book, this is not to criticise or blame any generation for what happens but instead to explain in practical terms why it does and show how it can be changed.

The key message of this book is that the solution to one set of problems brings with it a new set of challenges which require increasingly sophisticated and complex ways to manage them. Self-control is not easily learned and whilst the old adage says the 'absolute power corrupts absolutely', so it can be with great wealth – unless we learn the skills and abilities to handle it. Whilst many may find this hard to understand, the possession of wealth comes with limitations and suffering, as well as opportunity and many wonderful experiences. You can put up a shed in a day, but more complex structures take time, thought, planning, expertise and understanding. And to build something more complex, you need to have the awareness and ability. The accomplishment of one set of goals itself creates the need for a new set of abilities and the development of higher levels of skill in order to creatively and effectively work with what has been so effectively constructed.

In Chapter 5 we take a detour into some of the more philosophical understandings which underpin our approach, and this chapter is intended for those who want to know more about Ken Wilber and the theories behind integrating psychology, organisational management and social development. However, the book has been written so that Chapter 5 is not an essential read and the following chapters can be fully understood by those who are not as interested in this aspect.

In chapters 6 to 9, the book then sets out the specific generational issues facing families, looking at the first, second and third generations (onwards) and explaining the strengths and challenges for each and the areas which can be targeted in order to resolve the question of the three-generation wealth trap.

This book is intended to be both explanatory and problem-solving and includes key action points at the end of each chapter and suggestions for how to make changes. This includes, in Chapter 9, a template for a broad-based approach to helping younger generations develop an understanding of the value and opportunities that wealth provides, inspiring their own motivation and ambition and helping them to see their own potential, both personally and in relation to their families and the wider world.

There is a story which is often told of a man who had a grandson who was going to take over from him. When the grandson was getting married, the grandfather wanted to give him a blessing for success in his endeavours – but the grandson refused the blessing. He did so because he wanted to earn success from his own merit rather than rely on the blessing of someone else. As an older man, the grandson realised that he had been foolish – he could have taken the blessing and built upon it.

This book takes that story as its starting place and says that to be able to accept a blessing and understand the value of it, but not stop there and instead build upon it, is the key to long-term success both for individuals and for their families.

References

There are a number of books which help build a picture of current research and thinking in the field of neuroscience, behaviour and psychology. For those interested, this developing area of research looks at the neurological underpinnings of our emotions and behaviours, rather than just considering them to be learned behaviours which can be 'unlearned'. A sample, but by no means an exhaustive list, of these includes:

Berkman, E.T. (2012) 'The motivated brain: the brain's clues to finding a will and a way'. *Psychology Today*, November 22nd

Eagleman, D. (2011) *Incognito: The Secret Lives of the Brain*. New York, NY: Pantheon

Lieberman, M.D. (2013) *Social: Why our brains are wired to connect*. Oxford: Oxford University Press

Squire, L.R. (2013) *Fundamental Neuroscience*. Oxford: Academic Press

De Hann, M., & Gunnar, M.R. (Eds) (2011) *Handbook of Developmental Neuroscience*. New York, NY: Guilford Press

CHAPTER 1

The Root of the Problem

There is an ancient Chinese proverb which states '富不三代' (or 'Fu bu guo san dai'), which translates as 'wealth does not sustain beyond three generations'. It is sometimes expressed in English as 'rags to riches and back again in three generations', and in Arab culture, the three-generation phenomenon is described by Khaldun in *The Muqaddimah: An Introduction to History* thus:

> The first generation retains the desert qualities, desert toughness, and desert savagery ... they are brave and rapacious ... the strength of group feeling continues to be preserved among them. They are sharp and greatly feared. People submit to them.

> Under the influence of royal authority and a life of ease, the second generation changes from the desert attitude to a sedentary culture, from privation to luxury and plenty, from a state in which everybody shared in the glory to one in which one man claims all the glory ... others are [in] ... humble subservience ... the vigour of the group feeling is broken ... But many of the old virtues remain in them, because they had had direct personal contact with the first generation ...

> The third generation, then, has (completely) forgotten the period of desert life and toughness ... Luxury reaches its peak among them ... Group feeling disappears completely ... People forget to protect and defend themselves ... In the course of these three generations, the dynasty grows senile and is worn out.

The Family Business Institute estimates that 97% of family businesses do not survive past the third generation. Or at least, some of the businesses themselves may continue to exist, but they are no longer in the ownership of the family. In June 2011, Bloomberg Business Week ran an article about the 'Fall of the House of Busch', noting that it took four generations to build Anheuser-Busch, and only one generation for it to fall apart. The St Louis-based beer company that produces Budweiser survived Prohibition, labour strikes and price wars, growing to generate nearly $17 billion in revenue by 2008. But after failing to adapt to a changing market, the company was acquired by Belgian–Brazilian conglomerate InBev in a hostile takeover worth $52 billion.

Wealth professionals say it is not because of estate taxes or an inability to transfer the wealth that it often doesn't make it to the third or fourth generation. Instead, they often argue that it is an inability to transfer the knowledge of how to create it and how to keep it. However, we disagree with this and instead argue that knowing how to transfer and keep wealth is not a 'first-generation skill'. The first generation evidently know how to create it, but how to preserve and transfer wealth is not necessarily knowledge which they have a need to develop or possess. We believe that each generation of the family will encounter a variety of different circumstances relating to the family's wealth, and therefore the demands on the generations and the challenges they face are, inevitably, different. This is also affected by the individuals' different genetic and social realities.

It is therefore argued in this book that each generation needs to understand their 'stage' (taking into account their genetic, neurological and social realities) and develop appropriate skills, which the generation before does not necessarily possess or understand, to meet the challenges they face. In many ways, these different skills may appear to put them at odds with the previous generations and, if not understood, this can cause tension. For example, the preservation of wealth may require a more conservative and less entrepreneurial approach which the first generation (or those who watch and comment from the sidelines) may view as a sign that their children lack ambition or that they are guilty of 'complacency'. But perhaps the second generation lack that 'entrepreneurial gene' and instead have developed conservational skills and abilities, which are a combination of a number of influences.

To write off subsequent generations as 'less than' the initial wealth-creating generation is an unfair generalisation and, crucially, is fatalistic, implying that there is no way out of this trap. What we instead argue is that it is possible to break the 'rags to riches to rags' cycle but that this needs to be done by training and helping each generation to develop the skills which they need to have for the particular stage of the wealth cycle in which they are living. These are often not the skills which were needed by their parents or grandparents.

The three-generation cycle of wealth and loss is one which is global and is not specific to the twentieth and twenty-first centuries. As Khaldun expresses, there are underlying psychological and sociological reasons for this phenomenon. For example, the first generation may have created their wealth through a combination of intelligence, the right genetic composition, luck, skill and determination. However, this does not necessarily mean that they are going to pass these qualities effectively to the next generation, nor will the first generation necessarily have skills and abilities which allow them to do other things, such as preserve existing wealth effectively (as is expected of the second generation) or motivate themselves when there is no real need to do so (such as the third generation is required to do). With this in mind, there is a need to provide a solution, showing how developments in neurology,[1] linking to further thinking in psychology and behavioural science, can ensure a way out of the three-generation trap in a way which stops seeing an inevitable downward trend from the second generation onwards.

As an example, the three-generation story is often the (almost mythical) 'immigrant story' and is a common one in North America and Western Europe. The story goes like this: the first-generation immigrant works hard, almost non-stop, to build a foundation.

Everything they earn goes towards their children: their education and future. The second generation achieve or consolidate the goal of the parents, the first generation – but this was not their own goal. They create nothing new; they simply continue or solidify the achievements of their parents. In the case of immigrants, that goal is to reach that middle class or upper-middle class of mainstream society, one to which they were not allowed access due to their ethnicity and/or the poverty of their background. The narrative continues that the third generation, born into great comfort and luxury, do not know what it is like to struggle and work hard (but this was, of course, the direct intention of their grandparents). They are born with a sense of entitlement which is perhaps to be expected when a person grows up the way that they do. They expect things to be given to them or believe that they somehow deserve them. And this is when the decline happens.

In history, we see numerous examples of this, and the narrative of an inevitable three-generation decline. Take the Roman Empire. In a nutshell, the early Romans worked hard to establish Rome after the decline of Greece as the power in the Mediterranean. The history of the Gracchi and Marius details this and the building of the Republic of Rome, founded on great principles and ideas. In the second phase, or the 'second generation', so to speak, the Republic of Rome gradually changes into the Empire of Rome. Notable figures from this time include Sulla, Pompey, and Julius Caesar. By this time, Rome has grown so large that they need to find ways to control it and to stream-line operations and the administration of the various provinces and territories. This is the consolidation of the goals of the first generation – the second generation are the 'preservers of wealth', rather than the creators of it. The third generation is the decline phase. The emperors are not looking to expand the empire or improve it. The pure ideals are gone and, instead, they now look to line their purses or satisfy their whims. With prosperity comes corruption. Rome has now become so bloated that it starts to rot from within and a look at the histories of Nero, Commodus, and other bloody emperors attests to this.

In other words, even the narrative of the history of Rome can be seen to mirror the three-generation cycle. The first generation work hard to build something. The second generation may build upon it, but primarily aim to consolidate the goals of the first generation, and preserve them but do not innovate. The third generation, because they did not have the same experience of having to work hard, to struggle and to earn everything, inevitably fail to recognise the significance of the wealth (which is, to an extent, taken as a 'given') and lose it. This is, of course, a generalisation but it is, we feel, a relatively accurate one.

However, we argue that the three-generation cycle is not the inevitable outcome which it is so often assumed to be. Although embedded into our cultural psyche, it is possible to avoid the three-generation trap by recognising, firstly, that it is not a certainty, and secondly that it can be escaped through an understanding that we fall into the three-generation trap when we try to apply the same set of solutions to a different set of challenges. Whilst the second and third generations of a family are in a relatively privileged social and financial position compared to those of the first generation, and are required to 'thrive' rather than simply 'survive', they are also facing a more complex and very different set of 'life tasks', and a high level of psychological and socio-cultural development is required to meet the challenges they face. Each solution to a problem inevitably creates a more complex set of problems, although with less immediate or obvious difficulty.

Succession planning is as important in a family business as it is in a public corporation. Without it, the child who takes over the running of the business, either because he's the eldest or sometimes just because he is the one who lives closest to home, may not be the best qualified. Frequently, the family members who remain with the family business are the ones who return to the family business after school because it is the only place they can get a job. This is not how other businesses choose their employees.

But families can lose their wealth by the third generation even when a family business isn't involved. Sometimes, the second and third generations do not understand how to hold on to or create wealth. We argue that this is because they have not grown up with an understanding of the skills they will need to develop in order to thrive. Frequently, financial professionals will say that they have seen a first generation who create the wealth followed by a second or third generation who only know how to spend it. It perhaps does not help that the kind of personality that creates an enormous amount of wealth is often a larger-than-life, 'Type A' personality who likes to remain in control. It is probably not necessary to name names at this point as most people can usually think of someone who fits the bill!

The typical wealthy family often has a patriarch who has spent a great deal of time at work, because the fact is that ordinary people doing ordinary things with an ordinary level of effort is not what creates wealth. It is when people do extraordinary things that wealth can be created, and when that energy is put into work, something is often sacrificed at home. The generation who come after the wealth has been created are not always as diligent about saving or being careful of spending because, ultimately, they do not have to be. The children grow up believing they are going to inherit a significant amount of money, and this is probably because they are. Second-generation wealthy often lack savings and perhaps spend lavishly, but are still often making money themselves (either within the family business, or as individuals). The third and fourth generations, however, never even learn to save (which requires a level of awareness as to the potential uncertainty of the future, usually based on past experiences – either directly or indirectly received). They grow up entirely within that lavish lifestyle and therefore may not have the incentive or have developed psychologically in a way that would provide them with the motivation to either save or make more money.

What we argue, somewhat contrary to the narrative which is put forward in many quarters, is that it is not that somehow the third generations of wealthy families are inherently useless layabouts who lack moral fibre, intelligence or any sense of right and wrong! In the UK, the language used to describe wealthy second- and third-generation children who suddenly find themselves in the public eye is not dissimilar to the language used to describe benefits claimants (lazy, feckless, lacking moral courage etc.). At worst, second- and third-generation wealthy children are often directly compared with their high-achieving parents or grandparents. For example, the son or grandson of a first-generation wealth creator who is a successful businessman may find, at school, that he is 'expected' to be good at maths, at science or in whatever field in which his father or grandfather found success, and that he has to endure a raft of negative comments when his skills or interests lie elsewhere. This can be hugely damaging to a young person's sense of self-esteem and can be a significant barrier to motivation.

What we insist is that it is not that the second and third generations of wealthy families are inherently 'substandard' but instead that they need to be ready to meet a very different set of challenges from those which faced their parents or grandparents. They are not required to 'survive' but are instead expected to 'thrive' and to understand the value of hard work and ambition in an abstract way. The practical or monetary value of any efforts they make is not immediately apparent compared to the overall wealth of their families, and therefore we are expecting the third generation to be somehow able to see 'value' in ambition and endeavour that does not actually transform their lives in any practical sense. But the question we need to ask ourselves is whether many of us would understand the 'value of hard work' if there was not a direct link we could make between hard work and an improvement in our personal circumstances. If we experienced a world without this direct link, why would our brains wire and adapt to an entirely different set of circumstances without intervention? Here is the key issue of 'development' and how it happens.

Following World War II, a condition called 'hospitalism' (or 'hospital-ismus'), in which simply staying in hospital for long periods seemed to have an adverse effect on the physical and mental development of infants, was studied extensively. What was shown was that our environment as children has a direct impact on almost all aspects of our neurological development including language, social adjustment, neuromuscular development (even, for some, our height!) and, in some instances, acquired attitudes that are said to persist into adult life. What the study of hospitalism showed was that our environment, the stimuli we are exposed to, does not just affect our behaviour superficially, but instead actually changes our brain itself, causing it to be 'rewired' according to our environment. This wiring impacts upon all of our neurochemical balances including hormone production and the chemicals which stimulate our 'reward responses' such as dopamine.

Our environment and experiences can directly affect how the right hemisphere of our brain communicates with the left and how effectively the 'upper' or more sophisticated areas of our brain moderate our more primal impulses (such as anger). Whilst this 'rewiring' can continue well into adulthood, our most vulnerable (or, alternatively, our most potentially 'rich') time is as children or adolescents, which is the time when our brain structures are changing and growing the most with new pathways being laid down and consolidated at a huge pace.

We need to create environments which actively stimulate us neuro-logically, helping to 'wire' our brains in a way that leads us towards lives that are personally and socially rewarding – valuing ambition, stable relationships, philanthropy and, often, prioritising long-term over short-term satisfaction. And, due to the importance of the early years of childhood and adolescence for the establishment of these key neurological pathways, we can see why it is often so difficult for families to avoid the three-generation wealth trap – the interventions are often too little, too late and not aimed at addressing the right challenges. Behavioural interventions and the implementation of organisational changes can help – but we argue that where they are successful, it is because they have indirectly acted on the individual's neurological and corresponding psychological and behavioural structures, effectively rewiring these by 'accident'. Instead, our approach is targeted at these structures deliberately to ensure the greatest possible chance that the development will be measured, planned, enhanced and ultimately lead to success. This is because the 'development' part is key and what this book sets out are the reasons why other approaches often fail – not because they are not well-intentioned, but because they are aiming all their efforts at the wrong targets.

When we consider the life environments of many first-, second- and third-generation individuals, it is, from a neurological perspective, unsurprising that they struggle to develop certain skills or understandings and yet are so strong in others. In this book, we look at how to help create the optimal environment from a neurological perspective, starting with understanding the reasons why we develop the way we do.

We argue, in particular, that the challenges facing third generations of wealthy families are complex and we need to understand their place within a system of wealth which brings with it both privilege and obstacles to healthy psychological and social development. In other words, third-generation members of wealthy families are not like the majority of people in society who understand the need to get up in the morning to earn enough money to pay the mortgage and the bills. And so we cannot expect them to behave as such – if we want them to behave differently we need to enable the development of skills and abilities which will allow them to meet the complex challenges they face. The benefits of wealth are essentially like an inverted 'U' (as will be elaborated on later): increasing at first as wealth increases, then levelling off and eventually decreasing. Essentially, this is because the possession of extreme wealth, like the possession of extreme anything, is harder to cope with than average levels.

It is important to say, at this point, that this is not a textbook on neurology, nor is it intended as such. We reference neurological research and theories here for those who are interested in the more detailed neuroscientific studies which inform our current understandings. However, this book is for the layman who would like a greater awareness of the challenges they and their family may face, why this is the case, and how to plan and effect a response to that. Neurology – in particular the links between our neurological structures and our psychological development, and how these affect all other aspects of our lives – is a field of study which is still, in many ways, in the early days of its development. Therefore, this book is bound to be tweaked in the future as research guides us towards more in-depth understandings, but the intention here is to summarise the challenges and present the solutions in the best way they can be understood in the still-early days of the twenty-first century.

The challenges facing family businesses to succeed in the maintenance of long-term stability and growth, sustaining wealth over multiple generations, are fundamentally rooted in this three-generation phenomenon and how to address it. The relative lack of success in this area through the use of traditional models of wealth management and transfer has shown that a new approach is needed.[2]

This new approach is one which can overcome both internal and external threats to the survival and success of these enterprises. The approach proposed here meets the need for a more holistic, integral and broad-based model of investing, managing both the short-term and long-term needs of family businesses – and balancing the often competing needs of the family itself and the family's businesses which aim to provide for both present and future generations of the family. This is effectively a skills training process through which each generation of parents comes to understand where they are within the chain and recognise what their children will need to deal with the issues and challenges that they will face as a consequence of the family's wealth.

In order to explore these issues, in this chapter we shall consider:

a) Problems and challenges facing family businesses and the maintenance of wealth over multiple generations,

b) The four phases of the family business over multiple generations, and

c) The internal and external structures of the family business model

Problems and Challenges Facing Family Businesses

The 'family business' arguably has a contradiction inherent in its very structure and name. Considered as a whole, the family business is a composite of two distinct and often opposing components: the family or 'people' side, and the business or 'wealth' side.

As such, the family business can be seen as a psychological, social, philosophical, moral, ethical and financial entity and therefore is a far more complex model of wealth management than almost any other type of organisation. It is a family business and is therefore intended to meet the needs of the family who have been established as its beneficiaries, but what if the needs or wishes of that family, or the individual members of it, are not in line with the demands of sound long-term business or wealth transfer planning or management? In effect, we are using two competing models here (the business and the family) and there needs to be a more effective 'third model' which recognises the complexity of this issue and can effectively incorporate the other two when they come into conflict.

Consider, for example, the statistics regarding family businesses in the UK. Family firms make up nearly 76% of the 4.6 million private sector enterprises and nearly half of all mid-sized businesses in Britain. However, approximately only 30% of these firms operate into second-generation ownership.[3]

These are statistics which are repeated all over the globe, so are not a particularly UK phenomenon. There are, of course, numerous factors accounting for this, but dominant are issues of governance, succession planning, the disempowerment of younger generations, operational inefficiency or mediocrity, poor management systems, short-term thinking (e.g. not distinguishing between investments and expenses) and the subsequent difficulties in balancing financial and familial needs.

There are also, of course, external economic factors such as changing global trends and differing patterns of demand and growth which can significantly affect the success of long-term strategies for wealth preservation. Competition, changing markets and global events can wreak havoc on a financial strategy which may, at one time, have seemed infallible.

These external factors are one aspect for which successful family business management must be prepared, for example through innovation, diversification or investment in areas of business which may include gambling or alcohol enterprises (often 'rolled up' investments in the leisure industry).

And this is one area where we can see that what may seem a straightforward choice for an 'ordinary' business may present a challenge for many family businesses. For instance, a family business whose investments may include the ownership of commercial premises may, from a financial perspective, favour granting leases to a chain of betting shops whose recent performance on the high street has far outstripped many other businesses. But would investment in betting shops or other morally challenging enterprises be a decision supported by the individuals for whom the family business provides? Perhaps for some, yes, but perhaps for others, no. And so, even in this isolated and relatively simple example, the potential conflict between 'business' and 'family' is highlighted, and even a potential conflict between the members of the family who may have conflicting agendas, goals and needs.

The family business is, therefore, above all, an exercise in effective governance, of which wealth management is only one part and where social, ethical and psychological issues are of equal importance.

The Four Phases of the Family Office

To consider the changes to business structures over multiple generations, we are using, as an example, the 'family office'. A family office is essentially a family business, albeit a specific subset of family businesses, often centred around wealth management. However, the model here is applicable to all family businesses which are intended initially to provide for a patriarch or matriarch and their immediate family, needing to change and adapt to provide for future generations and often struggling to keep up with the increasing numbers of intended beneficiaries.

Family offices are usually defined as either single or multiple entities, serving either one family or many. However, we believe that they should more accurately be seen as having a four-stage life cycle which we set out below. The need is for the consultant to recognise both the current and the most appropriate stage for any particular family business structure. In order to identify the most successful strategies for management, it is essential firstly to know at what stage the family business is at the point where the consultant becomes involved and, secondly, at what stage the family business in question should be in terms of its natural life cycle.

There are challenges at each of the stages, including, for example, whether or not to split the wealth, which may sometimes be the optimal solution.

It is our position that these four stages are organic and unavoidable and, crucially, that for successful family business consultancy, professionals and family members need to acknowledge that the family business structure is dynamic and always in a state of change and development.

Stage 1: The Principal Family Office

The first stage is that of a principal family office (PFO) where the first-generation individual has successfully created the wealth but the family itself is still relatively small and compact, consisting of only one or two generations. At this point, the function of the family business is to serve the needs of the principal (including what may appear at face value to be the needs of his family, such as multiple homes dotted around the world, but which are essentially those of the principal himself). This PFO is, however, not yet structurally able or designed to meet the needs of multiple family members living separate lives. In this way, the PFO can be seen as the 'under one roof' family business structure.

The challenge for family offices as businesses at this initial stage is to manage the structural and philosophical changes necessary to develop into a single family office. The single family office is a different business entity which, although it may initially look similar at face value, has key differences. Failure to effectively manage the change from PFO to single family office in terms of the business structure can set up significant problems for the future.

A PFO is equivalent to a family-run business under the control of, and providing income for, one patriarch. In the PFO, there are no shareholders, no 'board' and no demands on the capital or profit of the business other than the operational needs of the business itself, and then those of the principal. Also the children and spouse are not important or taken into consideration in terms of running the PFO, either because of age or some other reason.

Stage 2: The Single Family Office

The function of the single family office (SFO) is to establish a family wealth or 'business' structure which is designed to meet the needs of the expanding family of the principal who have reached or are reaching a degree of independence. Whereas a PFO was adequate to meet the 'under one roof' needs of the family up to, and perhaps including, purchasing property for the principal's children to live in away from home, the family structure by this stage is becoming more complex. There are perhaps spouses and a third generation coming into existence, and a structure of wealth which comes directly through the principal to meet specific needs (often those of the principal's choosing) is no longer appropriate.

Whereas the PFO met the income needs of the second generation as children through meeting the needs of the principal, the structure is changing and the business now needs to meet those income requirements either through increased 'profit' which is then disseminated, or through giving the second- and then third-generation children an active role within the business in order that they can generate their own income. But through this expansion, the family office, as a family business, is changing in structure. It now has a number of people (albeit at this stage still a relatively small number) who wish to have some control over its operations. It has therefore moved into a business structure which, de facto, has 'shareholders' who are beneficiaries of the business and is under the control either of a single 'new' patriarch, whose responsibility it is to ensure all the 'shareholders' are provided for adequately, or of a board which fulfils the same role as the patriarch used to under the PFO structure. It is normally, though, still run by members of the family and has their direct involvement.

This change is essential, as the continued existence of a PFO structure when the family has become larger and now includes a third generation and those who have married into the family can cause two significant problems. Firstly, the centralisation of the wealth structure around the principal does not allow for the future security of the family's wealth. The principal retains control and, in this case, the likely outcome is that on the principal's death, the existing wealth will simply be divided between his children. In this way, the process of wealth dilution begins. If the principal has four children who each go on to have four children, an initial $80m held by the principal will be inherited (assuming nil growth or loss) as approximately $5m by the third generation. A nice inheritance perhaps, but a significant diminishment for the principal's grandchildren from those enjoyed by the principal and the first generation. This issue is often compounded by divorce and non-married partners, including same-sex partners.

Secondly, the continued existence of a PFO can cause substantial problems for the family relationships, with the risk of envy, demotivation amongst subsequent generations, resentment and over-reliance on the principal a significant feature of the failure to adapt from a PFO to an SFO.

Thus, the transition from PFO to SFO is crucial in ensuring that the process of wealth dilution is minimised and the multi-generational potential of the wealth realised by the principal is maximised.

However, some of the problems which arise at this point include issues relating to future planning and how the transition from principal to second-generation management is handled. What often occurs, with benefits and problems in equal number, is the transition to a second-generation patriarch whose responsibility becomes the management of wealth for both his own and his siblings' families. This structure is often preferred (or adopted by default) as it is the structure which is most similar to the PFO and therefore does not require significant organisational changes (other than, effectively, a change in personnel). An example of a different model to this is where a small 'board' of siblings run the businesses which were previously all managed by one patriarch.

Stage 3: The Multiple Family Office

Although a multiple family office (MFO) is often understood to be a family office structure where the wealth of different families is managed simultaneously, by the time the third and fourth generation of the principal's family is of age, the SFO has effectively become an MFO, either by choice or by default.

Assuming that most members of each generation marry and have children, the wealth of the principal which previously serviced the needs of one patriarch and four children now needs to provide for potentially upwards of sixty individuals, their spouses and their children. This is now a business with a larger number of 'shareholders', which of course means that the demands on the business to operate at a profit are significantly increased, but, in reality, the dividends received by the shareholders will, unless the business has undergone a phenomenal expansion within the last couple of decades, be substantially reduced. This is of course exaggerated where there are families with high numbers of children, for instance in religious Chassidic Jewish homes where eight to twelve children is often the norm.

By this stage, many of the families linked ancestrally with the original patriarch will have little or no direct relationship with the chairman of the family business and their connection to each other is becoming more distant. The issue which often arises at this stage is 'what is the continued purpose of the family office?' In essence, this is a turning point at which the purpose of the family office becomes the preservation of the business itself, and the meeting of the income needs of the family is a secondary gain of the business, rather than (as in previous phases) its primary goal. In general, as the generations develop, the emphasis on the business rather than the family becomes more pronounced.

The choice at this point for families is whether to continue with providing a relatively small but equal income for each of the existing family units or whether to consider separating the wealth into individual SFOs and essentially splitting the wealth into a number of parts. The risk at this point is that without careful management and governance, the family office as originally established will implode.

There is an underlying issue which is rarely addressed, which is 'just because a parent has money, does that mean the child automatically should inherit or that somehow it is theirs?' There is a movement started by Bill and Melinda Gates based on the idea that the ultra-wealthy should give away their money to philanthropic causes rather than let the next generation inherit it. Whatever is decided, the key is to be clear to the next generation what the plan is. We will explore this in future chapters.

Stage 4: From MFO to Asset Management

As with families such as the Rockefellers, by this point the members of the family for whom the principal's wealth is attempting to provide may number in the many hundreds, or even thousands.

These family business structures, if they survive the transition, essentially reduce most of the family members to shareholders in a corporation with very little ownership or control and, crucially, often a very small income from that association. The CEO running the company might well be wealthier than the family members.

There is, of course, within each extended family, the opportunity for a new 'principal' to emerge who successfully creates independent wealth, potentially using some of the income provided from the original family business. When this happens, the four-phase cycle begins again. If not, the role of the family business chair is essentially that of asset manager for a generic group of shareholders. This raises key structural questions for consultants, including personnel issues, governance and intention; as with the transition from SFO to MFO, the problem which arises is 'what is the function of the family business?'

There are, of course, pros and cons of both the MFO and asset management structures. A clear positive of asset management is that each family member will get a share, albeit a smaller share, of the family's wealth, and the asset management structure is better able to meet the needs of large groups of people, often geographically and sometimes culturally diverse.

On the negative side, however, the ownership of the family over the family's wealth and the direction of the business diminishes with each passing generation and whilst they receive some income from the business, it is not really what would be termed 'wealth'.

The Internal and External Structures of the Family Business

In essence, any family business (whether equivalent to a PFO, SFO or MFO) comprises four distinct component parts.

Firstly the individuals of the family in terms of their internal development psychologically and intellectually, and secondly the external or 'measurable' aspects of those individuals (for example, their IQ or cognitive ability, their health and their tangible, measurable personal or interpersonal skills). A combination of these first and second parts means that these individual members will have different internal and external capabilities and varied levels of development and self-awareness, due to both their age and their own personal potential.

Thirdly, these individuals are part of a society, community or culture which informs their internal realities as part of that cultural collective. Lastly, the family business exists as part of an external organisation or system and operates within these structures.

Psychology shows us that all individuals are likewise a complex mixture of these four components, internal and external, individual, societal and cultural.

To notice these different aspects as a way forward is to draw on the theories of Ken Wilber,[4] who has agreed that the four aspects, which he has termed 'quadrants', interact with one another and our development in each area will always be affected by the level of development of the others.[5]

As an example, if an individual lacks intellectual ability or a necessary organisational skill, he will struggle to master the skills necessary to manage a large business. The business he sets up or steps in to manage will likely be flawed in conception or execution, either in terms of its organisational structure or the governance which exists. The individual may have taken up the reins of the business through inheritance or marriage and may be at odds with the organisational culture within it.

If that individual ploughs money into that business, particularly if it is family money being used, this is likely to be unsuccessful and damage the relationships within his family through erosion of trust and confidence. This inevitably causes stress, which impedes our ability to function at an optimal level cognitively or emotionally and affects our behaviour, our ability to manage our relationships and our businesses appropriately, and so on.[6, 7, 8]

What this simple example shows is that the main reason family businesses struggle is that to consider only one aspect is a flawed approach. Experience shows that if all aspects are addressed in an integrated approach, the success of any endeavour is increased exponentially.

How to Begin to Resolve This

What run throughout this book are some suggestions for tasks and actions which will start the process of change for you and your family. These tasks are developmental in nature and geared around the key areas of self-awareness, awareness of those around you, identifying the challenges each generation will likely face, and how to address these challenges, step by step.

In relation to what has been discussed in this chapter, the best place to start is a family tree where you list each member of the family to whom this relates, and note whether they are first, second or third generation (plus). Once you have done this and started to think of the family members in terms of the generations to which they belong, you will be in a position to start thinking about their developmental needs and the challenges which they are likely to face in their lives – both personally and professionally.

Once you have a 'tree' for your family, make a note for each generation of the circumstances which surrounded them as they grew up. These would include whether or not their parents were working full time, the financial situation of the family during their own childhood and adolescence, and any other life experiences, either personal or those of the family or generation as a whole, which you feel may be influencing them either directly or indirectly. If you can, try to do this non-judgementally and without a sense of how 'easy' they have it, although this can be difficult, particularly when looking at third-generation individuals and comparing this to a different experience of life growing up. When this is done, try to think through the challenges you think they will face in their lifetime (including parenting the generation below!) and the skills you think they will need in order to overcome these.

In doing this task, you have started the process of the generational needs analysis, beginning to think of generations as different in experience and make-up and therefore needing different things from the generation before in order to help them to thrive.

Summary

We imagine that we would all like to have the 'problems' and challenges facing the second and third generations of a wealthy family. However, for many individuals, some of these challenges start with an assumption by the majority of people they meet (and many they will never personally meet) that they are pale imitations of their wealth-creating parent or grandparent. It is not an exaggeration to state that expectations of these individuals are often extremely (and frequently unfairly) high because of the 'privilege' of their backgrounds, which many assume (due to the lack of the ongoing financial struggles which the majority of people have to face) 'should' mean they are intrinsically happier, more capable, more emotionally and psychologically developed and more intellectually astute than the rest of society. These expectations are themselves a challenge for the individuals at the centre, both in terms of other people's expectations of them and, crucially, in terms of their own expectations of themselves.

One argument is that children are often brought up being told they are 'special' or 'clever' or talented in some way. Whilst the intention with this is admirable and only aimed at showing how much we value our kids, one of the unintended effects is that many children, particularly those from ultra-wealthy families, struggle to feel satisfied even if they do achieve, as it will always fall short of their own expectations of themselves (they are 'special', 'clever' and 'beautiful', after all …). 'If I am really that special or clever, surely I should have done more with my life?' That is the strange and unintended burden that many children carry forward into adulthood. We are not saying to stop the praise(!), but what we do advise is grounding that praise in actual achievements and encouraging realism which, as the child grows, enables them to develop a higher level of emotional intelligence. But more of this later …

What is often not recognised is that the very 'privilege' in which these children are raised brings with it a set of challenges which require solutions recognising that there are genuine external obstacles to their personal development, and the need is to understand and address these obstacles directly rather than wait for the child to fail and then criticise them for it. And we argue that even where this is recognised, it is not given enough priority. As we said in the introduction, the three-generation wealth trap is entirely avoidable, but it takes significant thought, planning and effort and it must be more than an afterthought.

This is what the underlying issues are, this is where others have gone wrong, and the rest of this book sets out these issues in detail, explaining how to address them at each stage and for each generation of a family to help both the individuals and the family's businesses thrive beyond the third-generation trap.

Chapter 1 – A quick reference guide:

1. The three-generation trap is avoidable if we know why it happens.

2. We need to think of each generation individually rather than assuming they are the same – they will have had different experiences which will have set up fundamental alterations in their neurological structures, their psychology and their personal abilities and challenges.

3. Sustaining wealth and business success over multiple generations requires changing approaches to short-term management and success.

4. We need to recognise the needs of the individual family members as well as the stage and needs of the family office as a whole with a thorough analysis. Then we can work out where there are similarities and differences in the generational and individual expectations.

5. Education is key – learning about the individual challenges facing each generation and understanding them will help to develop the skills that the different generations need for their stage.

6. Write a list of the members of the different generations in your family and make a note of the different experiences they have had growing up. Try to do so non-judgementally and notice how much the experiences of the second and third generations differ from those of the first etc. This will give you an idea of what you are dealing with.

7. When you have carried out point 6, write down what skills you think they have needed previously, and what skills you think they will need to meet the challenges they are going to face. We will come back to this later in the book.

Notes and References: Chapter 1

[1] Eagleman, D. (2011) *Incognito: The Secret Lives of the Brain*. New York, NY: Pantheon.

[2] An approach to the management of family offices which draws on the most advanced thinking in international finance, economics, philosophy and psychology is one which is grounded in the philosophies of Ken Wilber (2000; 2001), who argues that in order to maximise success, health and stability and to achieve our potential, either as organisations or as individuals, we must consider all aspects of both our internal and external worlds, and how these interlink and inform the development of other aspects.

[3] International Centre for Families in Business: http://www.icfib.com/education-and-research/?/facts-figures.

[4] For example, his 1996 work *A Brief History of Everything*.

[5] This understanding is best set out by Wilber, whose approach is to define the different aspects of our internal and external worlds into four 'quadrants' and, within these quadrants, to consider the level of development achieved. No aspect of our existence is outside the schema and all aspects are relevant to the success of any endeavour, whether professional or personal. For further discussion and a full explanation of Wilber's influence on the integral approach to consulting and management of family offices and wealth, please see Chapter 5.

[6] Berkman, E.T. (2012) 'What is the value of self-control? The intriguing link between self-concept and self-control'. *Psychology Today*, November 5th.

[7] Berkman, E.T. (2012) 'Goals, motivation and the brain: what can neuroscience tell us about how to succeed at our goals?' *Psychology Today*, November 12th.

[8] Berkman, E.T. (2012) 'The motivated brain: the brain's clues to finding a will and a way'. *Psychology Today*, November 22nd.

CHAPTER 2

Whose Money Is It Anyway?

Do you see differences between the generations in your family in terms of motivation, ambition, ability and expectations? Do you feel that the younger generations seem to have a sense of entitlement and are you frustrated by their apparent lack of drive or appreciation for the value of things – wondering when they will 'man up' and take the reins? Or, alternatively, do you feel that your parents' views on work and money are impossible to live up to and that they don't seem to understand that you feel differently about careers or business from them?

Following on from the issues which we set out in Chapter 1, and as highlighted by the International Centre for Families in Business, one of the main issues for family businesses is difficulties relating to the successful maintenance of wealth through multiple generations, and the passing of operational control to those successive generations. It is, as we said in Chapter 1, an issue of how to transfer the knowledge of both how to *create* wealth and how to *preserve* it.

In this chapter we demonstrate the main problems for each generation in terms of individual expectations, skills and expertise as well as cultural expectations and norms. We also set out an innovative and multi-faceted approach to dealing with these problems, including an awareness of the internal and external factors which create difficulties for successful longer-term wealth management.

This chapter tells the story of Robert, a businessman who, in his late seventies, found himself facing issues relating to ensuring the continued success of his enterprises and thinking about the longer-term intentions for his family's wealth.*

In telling this story, we are looking at common areas of difficulty for families which include generational differences, cultural considerations, the position of women and those who have married into the family, the individuals involved, the health of family relationships, the relative centralisation of the family business around one member, ethical and religious values, and, crucially, the key question: '*Whose money is it anyway?*'

By this, what we mean is the question of inheritance and 'ownership', and of what purpose the money is intended to serve. The first generation make the money, but whose is it? Does it belong to the subsequent generations by right, or not? And if yes, which members of the subsequent generations? By generation four, the number of members of that family will likely have increased tenfold (at least!). This is a key question which needs clarifying for any family business or family office, if there is to be successful multi-generational wealth transfer.

In chapters 7 to 9, we look more at the difficulties and potential solutions for each generation, but in this chapter, we start with considering many of these issues through an overview of a typical family office at a point of transition from the first to successive generations.

Background – The Patriarch

Although he was in his late seventies when he came to us, Robert was, in many ways, as much of a force to be reckoned with as he was in his early twenties. He grew up in New York and was one of the younger

---

* Included here is a composite of our work with various family businesses, drawing from a range of different examples. Therefore any similarity to a specific individual or particular family is entirely coincidental, but this story is intended to be indicative of some of the key questions which we encounter.

siblings of a large family of Italian ancestry, whose father, after spending a lifetime in various manual jobs, passed away when Robert was in his late teens.

From an early age, Robert knew that he did not want to spend his life doing physical work for very little financial reward, the way that his father had, and he determined early that he wanted to go into business. Having gained experience through his teens, by his early twenties he owned three expanding businesses and had bought his second house. The first house he had bought had been for his mother and younger siblings. At the age of twenty-nine, by then with four children of his own, Robert had made his first million dollars and was employing over 250 people, including two of his own brothers.

As an individual, Robert was fiercely bright and driven to succeed, with a natural instinct for when a business idea would work and when it would not. At the same time, he had struggled to decentralise his commercial operations and, as he approached his eightieth birthday, he remained at the helm of his various enterprises which, over the past sixty years, had been structured around him, his abilities and his interests.

The family's wealth was mainly in four areas: property, commercial interests, investments (including relatively low-interest deposit accounts), and held in trust in settlements established in the 1960s.

The Problems – Relational and Structural

Robert's eldest daughter, Josephine, had become increasingly concerned that the future security of the family's wealth was in doubt. She recognised that all roads led back to Robert, who, although still active and able, was starting to slow down. She was becoming increasingly frustrated by the difficulties that her brothers had expressed, and that she had witnessed directly, in sustaining the businesses: difficulties that came about as a consequence of the total centralisation of operations around their elderly father. At the same time, he refused to take a back seat. Her brothers struggled to persuade him on this and the relationships between her brothers and their father were suffering as a consequence. Josephine acknowledged that the global economic issues of 2008 onwards had also contributed to problems, but she understood that the family's overall wealth had contracted by approximately 30% over the past five years.

Of his children, the two boys, Thomas and Edward, had grown up in their father's shadow and, although competent businessmen in their own right, they were now in their fifties and had never been given independent control of any of the family's many operations, nor independent control of their own wealth. They received an income from the businesses through a combination of salary and dividends and were also beneficiaries of trust income, from the settlements established in the 1960s. The brothers were both beneficiaries, as were their own children, but the situation was becoming more complicated as the next generations emigrated to countries other than the USA, including the UK, Australia and France, with potential implications for the taxation of the settlement and the individual beneficiaries, meaning the settlements were not working as effectively as they had twenty years before. Both brothers were frustrated by their lack of control and, as they approached their sixties, could not see a future where they had any significant influence over the direction of the commercial operations. As a consequence, they had become more estranged both from each other and from their father, something which caused their mother upset and, apart from the damage to family relationships, was also impacting on the efficiency of the businesses.

Josephine was the most like her father and was as intelligent as she was capable, recognising that although the current state of the family's wealth was not at crisis point, she had correctly identified that problems were coming more and more to the surface. Due mainly to cultural norms, Josephine, despite her abilities, had never taken an active role in the family's commercial interests and her husband, Max, whom she married young, had become far more involved than she. Her husband had come from a similar Italian-American cultural background but was not from a wealthy family and at times felt the need to over-assert himself. In discussions, he came to recognise that this was mainly due to insecurity as to his position within the family which was, of course, entirely dependent on his relationship with Josephine, something he resented despite the relative health of their relationship overall. At the same time, Josephine had excelled in charitable work, assisting in the direction of the family's various philanthropic ventures although, like her brothers, she had never been given independent control of directing these activities.

The other sister, Robert's younger daughter, was not keen to be directly involved in the process and her husband, who was an artist and film-maker, had never expressed an interest. The work therefore needed to be concentrated on Robert, his wife Maria, his sons Thomas and Edward, his eldest daughter Josephine and her husband Max.

Starting to Resolve the Problem

It is always necessary to undertake an initial assessment of the situation, including looking at the family's business structures and systems, areas of strength and weakness, the values of the family and cultural considerations, not to mention considering the individuals involved and their own personal abilities, both emotionally and rela-tionally. This assessment takes place over a number of sessions with the different members of the family and includes thorough reviews of the businesses, investments and personnel.

At the end of this process for Robert and Josephine, a plan needed to be set out and agreed with the family, detailing the reasons for the difficulties currently being experienced, in terms of both the commercial structures and the family relationships, and laying out the likely development of the family's wealth over the next thirty years on the basis of the current situation versus a restructured family wealth transition process. Crucially, the emphasis needed to be on the importance of the family developing the human interaction skills necessary to run a successful family business.

Part of this assessment was to gain an answer to the crucial question 'whose money is this anyway?', helping to clarify that defining it as 'the family's wealth' was insufficient. Robert's family had access to the wealth but no ownership over it. Thought also needed to be given to what was meant by 'the family', which was growing in number and growing more separate in terms of relationships, and to the extent to which the different members were to be involved or provided for.

Key to the question of ownership was enabling Robert to see that whilst he had grown the family wealth over the past sixty years from nothing, he was giving mixed messages as to who it belonged to – in theory it belonged to all, but in reality it remained under his direction and absolute control. This strategy is ultimately a 'two-generation' approach, where the first generation centralise control during their lifetime but planning for after this generation has died is not a consideration. Passed to the children (the second generation), wealth is rarely sustained beyond that generation. Crucially, this is a problem which is bound to increase as we live longer – consider Prince Charles and Queen Elizabeth. If the current health of the monarch continues, Prince Charles will likely not inherit the throne until he is into his seventies.

It is important to recognise that thinking about what happens after our death is often a difficult subject and one which causes anxiety, but it is key to multi-generational security of family wealth, and our clients are encouraged to think well beyond their own lifetimes if their intention is to sustain wealth beyond their own children's generation.

In order to address this, in addition to the question 'whose money is it anyway?', it is also important to ask the questions 'what is money' and 'what is money used for?' We hold that money and 'wealth' are more than a surplus of financial assets. Our approach is that money and wealth are beyond this, enabling freedom and choice but also coming with responsibilities, both personal and social, and creating complexities which can cause tensions and relational difficulties. Although the issues regarding wealth are different to those which arise for those people who are without it, for our clients they are no less (and often more) complex and, in many ways, they require wealthy individuals to function at a higher level emotionally, relationally and socially than the average person. For example, it is often the case that the social and personal limitations which are put on others with average or below-average levels of wealth do not apply for our clients. Their choices are instead decided less by practical financial restrictions and more by their own personal values and their own emotional intelligence, which can put additional strain on them as individuals and on their relationships.

The question 'what do you want to achieve in your life?' also has particular resonance for individuals with wealth, as many of their primary, practical needs have been adequately met. Therefore, where does future ambition come from and for what purpose?

This is an issue which often arises when the first generation of a family describe their worries about future generations. They express concerns that the later generations are 'lazy' or that they appear to lack motivation, by comparison, of course, to their own ambitions and work ethic. We often find that we need to help these individuals, such as Robert, understand that the next generations are not 'lazy', but that their needs and therefore their aspirations will be different. In developmental terms, all humans are designed to take a risk only if the perceived reward is motivational. For those individuals in deprived, drought-stricken parts of the world, the question is 'why would I walk twenty miles for food when I will use more energy than I will replace?' For those individuals from backgrounds of wealth, the cost/benefit balance is related more to questions higher up Maslow's hierarchy of needs,[1] for example, issues of self-esteem. However, these issues are still pressing. For example: 'why would I work a sixty-hour week for £35,000 a year as a trainee solicitor, feeling de-skilled and risking that I will not be hired on qualification, when I receive four times that amount already from my trust with no risk involved?' or 'I've never believed I would have got this job if it wasn't the family's business and I think everyone else feels that way too'.

We believe that the questions outlined above regarding the perception of money, the perception of ownership, the purpose of wealth and the issue of individual aspirations are key to structuring a healthy and successful family business. Importantly, though, these are questions which are often answered differently by each individual and by each generation, and this is why the individual and multi-generational approach is key, alongside consideration of the family business as a whole.

The Individuals and the Relationships

With Robert's family, work needed to be focused initially on building an understanding of the issues and addressing how to resolve tensions within the family in order to establish trust and effective communication of concerns.

This would include individual and group work with Thomas, Edward, Max and Robert looking at their current situation and their aspirations, both personally and in terms of the family's businesses. The relational stage was essential in that, if Robert was to agree to the restructuring of his family's wealth and assets, it was critical to build trust and awareness of the capabilities, strengths and weaknesses of both himself and those to whom he would be handing over control.

First-Generation Issues

Issues for Robert as to what 'retirement' might mean to him on a personal level were a factor, as were the expectations of Thomas, Edward and Max. Initially, Robert favoured the continuation of the current structure of the business, but with Thomas nominally at the head of the family business. As with many first-generation individuals, Robert's personality made him reluctant to consider doing it differently and he found it very difficult to consider a time when he would take more of a back seat. Engaging Robert in the process was, in the early stages, part of the battle to help the family.

It was essential that what happened was not simply a handing over of control to one of Robert's children but a restructuring that would see the family's wealth grow and sustain well into the third generation and hopefully beyond. What Robert initially favoured, with Thomas taking over control, was essentially a replication of the current situation with centralised control under a single patriarch and did not address the relational issues within the family, ensuring that these would likely arise and hinder the work of the family business in the near future.

In answering the question 'what is money?', Robert was in many ways typical of the wealthy first generation who have come from nothing and created a large commercial operation which is self-sustaining. When asked this question, Robert smiled wryly and answered that 'money' was something that he still worried he would be without, and admitted that he still did not feel 'wealthy'. Although his experience of growing up without money had been more than half a century ago, Robert, unlike his children and grandchildren, came from a background where money was not something which could be taken for granted and 'wealth' was something almost entirely abstract.

It is a similar position to J.K. Rowling, who, in a recent interview, stated that 'To this day, I don't take it for granted that I can pay my bills, and that I can keep my house. It may sound improbable, but even today I take nothing for granted.'[2]

Another demonstration of this attitude comes from when J.K. Rowling was interviewed in 2010 by another self-made billionaire, Oprah Winfrey, where the conversation went as follows:[3]

Winfrey: Are you in a place now where you can accept that you will always be rich?

Rowling: No. Are you?

Winfrey: Kind of. Getting there.

Rowling: Really? I hope I . . . that sounds good . . . And you feel – I feel – I don't want to get complacent.

Winfrey: Right.

Rowling: I don't want to take things for granted.

This conversation speaks volumes about first-generation wealth-creators and, for Robert, this attitude was a key reason why he struggled to step away from his businesses as he approached his eighties and also why he struggled to understand the needs and desires of the next generations. He worried that future generations would not share his values and did not understand 'work ethic', so, alongside an intrinsic lack of feeling 'wealthy' and a sense of insecurity at being out of direct control of his businesses, Robert sought to lead by example. However, what developed was an attempt to demonstrate 'from the top down' what a work ethic is and what expectations his children should have of themselves without an understanding of their very different life experiences, goals and personal ambitions.

Although leading by example is important, what is missed with this approach is other individuals' own developmental history and how their understandings and ambitions are formed.[4, 5] Mimicking a parent or grandparent may work for a while, but the foundations of the motivation will be different and need to be found by the individual for themselves through an understanding of their own circumstances and through answering for themselves the questions we have set out above.

Working with Robert

Robert, as an individual, needed to look at his personal concerns and future ambitions, both for himself and for the businesses he operated. Part of this was recognising that the transition of the business into the control of the second generation was only part of the process for him. As mentioned earlier, Robert was initially sceptical about this change management process and could often be quite authoritarian with us as we tried to investigate the situation.

A significant issue for him was likely to be his own transition into retirement, which needed careful planning and a setting of motivational and achievable goals. Robert had spent his entire life in a process of planning for the future and working towards defined outcomes. To recommend that he spend the next decade in a state of (albeit, we could argue, well-deserved) idleness would have been in complete contrast to the way he had spent his life. Therefore the transition to retirement, and retirement itself, were things which needed to continue to reflect Robert's personality and ambitions as they had manifested throughout his life.

Robert did not want to be fully retired but still wanted to play a semi-active role in the businesses as long as he was able to do so, recognising that, at least for now, the idea of total non-involvement in his businesses was not something he wanted (at all!). Robert needed therefore to shape a future role for himself within the family's commercial enterprises that was realistic and defined and would not prevent the businesses from developing whilst still allowing him, during his lifetime, to have input into the future directions the businesses were to take. Part of shaping this role, however, was considering his expectations regarding the level of control he would continue to have and coming to recognise situations when he would need to, in his words, 'back off and leave them to it'. When he was satisfied with the defined role, considering his motivations for continuing work and what would be in the best interests of both himself personally and the companies as a whole, he would then be able to consider how best this role could be incorporated within the restructuring of the companies, in collaboration with the second generation.

Alongside this, however, Robert needed to consider where his other interests lay, and this revealed a long-held passion to build an internship programme enabling promising young men and women from difficult backgrounds to gain experience in business. Coming from the background he did, this project had personal significance for Robert and he was passionate about it. This was something he had started several times but his other commitments had meant he could not be as hands-on as he would have liked and the programme had, in Robert's words, developed into a standard work-experience programme accessing candidates from universities and colleges locally, rather than the mentoring and combined skill- and esteem-building experience, sourcing candidates from more challenging backgrounds, that he had wanted. Discussing how he could put the increase in his spare time towards enhancing and developing a programme such as this which had real meaning for him altered his attitude towards retirement on a personal level.

It would also be necessary to work with the second and, where appropriate, the third generations to address the other concerns held by Robert about the future of the companies when he had taken himself out of his central role.

Second Generation

In order to consider careful but thorough restructuring of the family's wealth for the third generation and beyond, Robert, Thomas, Max and Edward's relationships and their ability to resolve tensions needed to be fully developed. The process should always start with the individual and the relational before considering the external and structural issues relating to the wealth itself.

Individually, it was important to work with Thomas, Edward and Max as well as Robert, helping them to develop their own capacity and, for all three of the second generation, to find their own worth. For Thomas and Edward, a lifetime in their father's shadow had reduced their confidence that they could actually manage the family business and created a frustration that Robert seemed to believe the only way to manage things was 'his way', whilst for Max, his struggle was coming to terms with his own value to the family, both personally and as a businessman.

In our work with him, Max, in particular, was enabled to become more aware of his approach to the family's wealth and understand that his refusal to communicate his concerns to Josephine was perceived as withholding. Max came to understand that he had been overcompensating for feelings of insecurity through an attitude which appeared at times secretive and at others arrogant. Our work with Max, who represents the archetypal 'outsider' to the family, was key and centred around his own self-awareness, and others' awareness, of his capabilities and strengths.

For Thomas and Edward, as with Max, the work was essentially that of executive coaching on a personal level, but also assisting with rebuilding the relationships between them and the other family members, alongside helping to shape and develop their own personal goals, and defining 'family' ambitions. As is often the case, the three men engaged differently with the process – Edward being more committed and ready to embrace change than his brother, who was slightly more reluctant and cautious. But part of this process is to recognise the different personalities of the individuals, and to work with them to build on their own strengths.

Thomas, Edward and Max needed to consider the questions of 'what is money?' and 'what is money for?' alongside consideration of the question 'what do you want to achieve in your life?'

The difficulty for this generation is one expressed by Andrew Carnegie, who expressed his concern that 'the parent who leaves his son enormous wealth generally deadens the talents and energies of the son, and tempts him to lead a less worthy life'.

When heirs receive money without prior coaching on the purpose of money, it may be that they do not fully understand the values that helped accumulate the value of the inheritance. Inheritors, certainly from the perspective of the person passing the wealth, do not appear to understand the 'blood, sweat and tears' which were invested in building the wealth. Nor do heirs with money have the same need, and therefore the same motivation, as previous generations to develop diligence, delayed gratification and thrift.

Heirs may lack the meaningful pursuits needed to cultivate self-esteem, self-worth, motivation, self-confidence, and personal identity. Moreover, the vacuum created by the lack of a healthy purpose can lead to negative, often contradictory, outcomes, such as the inability to delay gratification, unwillingness to tolerate frustration, feelings of failure, arrogance and a false sense of entitlement.

As such, plans for Thomas, Max and Edward on an individual level involved a focus on purpose, motivation and identification of ambitions as well as enhancing their awareness of their own skill sets and achievements. Structurally, the extent to which they held similar cultural values needed to be thought through, and lastly they had to consider the parts they were best suited to play in the evolving family business.

The initial focus needed also to be on relationship-building. This was based on our understanding that good, healthy relationships between those individuals who are to take the family business into the next stage are essential for its success.

For Thomas, Edward and Max, the outcome was an understanding not only of their own skills but of those of the others, and a developing relationship of trust between them. They all developed the ability to 'respond' rather than 'react' to situations and to each other, enabling the family business to deal with potential tensions in a forum which balanced the needs of the individuals with the needs of the business.

Josephine was keen to take more direct control over the philanthropic arm of the family business, and our work with Robert, Josephine, Max, Thomas and Edward centred on taking her seriously as well as taking seriously the work which she proposed to do rather than seeing it as peripheral. This fitted with Robert's plans for retirement and the interests and personalities of Josephine and Robert were a particularly good fit, ensuring that each found purpose and value in the work which was to be done.

Decision-Making, Accountability and Governance

Once relationships have been developed between the family members, and between the family and external consultants or other professionals, the questions relating to what the family want for the future are clarified and agreed upon.

In this case, all members were keen to preserve the wealth for future generations and the best way forward for them was a more collaborative approach, rather than the strictly hierarchical one which had existed to date. Within this, the decision-making processes within the family business needed consideration before any actual restructuring took place, and so it was important to spend time with the key members of the family discussing and implementing a decision-making process which would be effective and would allow for both flexibility and, crucially, accountability within the family business.

All members by this stage would have recognised that, although they were implementing changes for Thomas, Edward and Josephine's generation of the family, the changes would be most crucial for the next, third, generation, by which time Robert would most likely have passed away and the decentralisation of the family business would have taken root.

Consideration of the third generation, some of whom were already in their early thirties, was important but needed to be deferred so as to ensure effective structures for decision-making and accountability were in place before any other members of the family were included.

With an effective, agreed decision-making process in place, the family business had an accountability and governance system which would enable further changes to be made. Underlying this, of course, were the improved relationships between the key family members as well as a developed sense of their own place within the system. With this decision-making process in place, Thomas, Edward and Max would be able to demonstrate to Robert their capability which, in turn, would enable him to take a further step back and allow the restructuring of the family's businesses and other assets into a family business fit for the twenty-first century (and hopefully beyond) to take place.

Restructuring for the Future

With a decentralised decision-making process alongside a strong system for accountability now in place, it would be possible to work through the businesses and assets and reshape the structure of the family's wealth, taking advice from appropriate experts and employing the best personnel to assist with this.

If this had been undertaken prior to the development of the family's interaction skills, the process would likely have ground to a halt at this stage. The creation of healthy systems for the business of a family business is dependent on a healthy family system in that the external systems often mirror the internal family systems, taking on flaws as well as strengths. Robert's family had clearly agreed their aims and the individuals continued to take responsibility for their own selves as well as their part in the family system. As a consequence, it was possible to establish a healthy business structure which reflected this.

This included considering whether the established trusts were being managed optimally, as well as looking at the fixed assets held by both the settlements and the businesses. The businesses had not been scrutinised in this way for decades and it was decided by the family that flexibility and the possibility for growth and expansion were as important as security and the preservation of the core wealth.

Part of this process was consideration of the third generation, and the intention was to incentivise and enable a sense of ownership amongst Robert's grandchildren and their partners, rather than of dependency. The systems put in place aimed to work towards this, intending to give the individuals a feeling of involvement in their own family's wealth and business, whilst also preparing those with the capacity for future leadership.

The Third Generation and Beyond

The third generation of Robert's family was a typical mix of the business-minded, the ambitious, the intelligent, the unmotivated and the less capable. Amongst the children of Josephine, Thomas and Edward, and their children's spouses, were a number of entrepreneurial personalities, an accountant, a university lecturer, as well as a golf pro and a ski instructor, students and a number of adult individuals who were yet to ever have taken a paid job.

The tendency of particularly third-generation wealthy to struggle to find purpose and value in business is to be expected, and it is often the case that some of the more negative outcomes of inherited wealth which are present for the second generation can become even more marked as we move down the family tree.

The need with regard to the third generation and future planning for the family business is to identify future leaders, but also to decide to what extent the members of the family are to be provided for going forward.

The questions here of 'what is wealth?' and 'what is money for?' are pertinent with respect to the third generation's expectations. For Robert, money was to provide a level of comfort and access to opportunities that would otherwise have been denied to him and his children. These opportunities included education and housing. Also, importantly, for Robert wealth represented a degree of freedom – in particular the freedom from having to take a job without prospects or social value purely to provide for necessities. However, there had never been an intention on Robert's part, or that of his own children, that wealth should mean there was no need to ever consider working, or that it should enable one to live a life without purpose or where the value of the individual to their society was not an issue. As such, it was decided that the family business would concentrate its provision for future generations on educational trusts with the intention of setting up a 'Bill Gates' model of wealth transfer (see Chapter 4 for further discussion on the models of wealth transfer).

Maintenance

Once the restructuring processes have taken place, the consultant's involvement tends to lessen with time. However, maintenance of the relationships, particularly as new members of the family come of age and their involvement increases, is crucial.

Summary and Analysis

The case of Robert's family business is intended to highlight some of the key issues faced by family businesses in attempting to secure wealth over multiple generations. Areas which we did not expand on here include the difficulties faced by the third generation, who, we often find, struggle to feel a sense of ownership and control in relation to the family business. Unintentionally, what is established by previous generations is a culture of dependency and a lack of motivation to succeed. This is often the reason that difficulties in sustaining wealth beyond the third generation are so prevalent within family businesses, and is a key issue which the integral approach seeks to address. The 'third-generation issue' is one which we shall consider more fully in Chapter 9, as it is one which it is important to discuss as a distinct and critical question.

The difficulties facing each generation and the solutions to these problems (discussed more in chapters 7 to 9), as well as the issues for 'outsiders' who marry into the family or for families where wealth is unexpectedly inherited, are distinct. Our approach has shown that the individuals, their relationships and their place within the family business system are as key to the success of the family business as the commercial structures and investments themselves. As set out in this case study, crucial to this success are human interaction skills, without which any venture will ultimately fail due to consequent difficulties in establishing effective communication of concerns, a lack of transparent and effective decision-making processes, and, critically, a lack of accountability. Accountability and decision-making, along with the ability to both see what is needed in the present and plan for the future, are key factors in the success of a family business, and the importance that an integral approach gives to the human elements within the family business, both individual and relational, is due to the fact that a family business without a healthy family system underlying it is bound to fail.

Chapter 2 – A quick reference guide:

1. The question 'whose money is it anyway?' is key to any planning or success long-term. This question needs to be resolved before any meaningful changes can happen. If we don't know the answer to this question for a family, then how can there be any understanding of what they want to happen and what is possible?

2. Each generation of a family needs to be focused on its particular needs, abilities, strengths and areas of development. Failing to recognise the difference between first, second and third generations (et al.) of a family will prevent any real growth or change.

3. As well as consideration of the individual family members' needs, a family office or business cannot work successfully without strong governance and future planning. Understanding how decisions are made, by whom and why is essential and must happen at an early stage.

4. Write down what you personally feel should happen to the family's wealth over the next few generations. What would you like to see happen? When you have done this, think about how likely this is to happen with things set up as they are at present, and what you think needs to happen to improve the chances of success (both for the office and for the individuals). If several members of the family do this, you have the starting point for a helpful discussion about the family's governance and future direction.

Notes and References: Chapter 2

[1]   Oleson, M. (2004) 'Exploring the relationship between money attitudes and Maslow's Hierarchy of Needs'. *International Journal of Consumer Studies*, 20(1), pp. 83–92

[2]   Spiegel (2012) 'SPIEGEL Interview with J.K. Rowling'. http://www.spiegel.de/international/zeitgeist/spiegel-interview-with-author-j-k-rowling-a-857632-2.html

[3]   *The Oprah Winfrey Show*. ABC, October 1st 2010

[4]   Berkman, E.T. (2012) 'Goals, motivation and the brain: what can neuroscience tell us about how to succeed at our goals?' *Psychology Today*, November 12th

[5]   Berkman, E.T. (2012) 'The motivated brain: the brain's clues to finding a will and a way'. *Psychology Today*, November 22nd

CHAPTER 3

The Psychology (and Neurology) of Money

What is 'money'? And what does it mean for us? How does the possession of wealth affect the way our brain wires itself in relation to ourselves, our families and the world around us?

What the possession of wealth shows us is that the solution to every problem also creates another problem – one which is perhaps less immediate, but one which is far more complex and so requires more sophisticated solutions. The answer to that problem can also never be found by using the solution which helped to solve the problems of the previous level of need. A new set of solutions is needed for each level of development as we move up Maslow's 'hierarchy of needs' (discussed later in this chapter). In Chapter 2 we saw how the challenges and needs faced by the first-generation Robert were not the same as those facing his children or grandchildren. Nor were the second and third generations' life experiences and expectations similar enough to each other to enable them to just 'carry on' with the family businesses as they were established. Due to these different experiences, their entire neurological structures were different – so why would we expect them to feel, act or prioritise in the same way?

However, an important aspect of all of this is the actual psychology of money itself. The psychology of money, how we understand it and respond to it, is key in being able to explain why wealth can create as many problems as it solves – albeit of a different nature. Therefore, in order to consider the psychology of money, the associated problems and the solutions, what we need first is to understand what 'money' is. And the answer is not as straightforward as we might think.

What Is 'Money'?

'Money', of and by itself, is nothing. It may be a stone, a coin, a piece of paper, but its value has absolutely nothing to do with the actual value of the object. Its only value is the value placed on it by society.

In a simple example, the value of 'money' is shown by the situation in Zimbabwe. Famous for its desperate economic crash leading to the notorious billion-dollar notes, Zimbabwe has been using a variety of foreign currencies since approximately 2009, none of which are its own. The Zimbabwean dollar is worth nothing, and instead prices in shops are shown in either US dollars or South African rand. This is a clear illustration that money is worth only the value we give it and that 'money' is essentially an abstract concept, rather than a purely concrete 'thing'.

Therefore 'money', as a concept rather than as a 'thing', has three key characteristics. It works as a medium of exchange, it is an economic 'good' and it is a means of economic calculation.

In order to really understand our relationship with money, both individually and culturally, it is helpful to understand how that relationship has developed over time.

The History of Money

Money as we know it has been in use for approximately the past 3,000 years, before which a bartering system was, it is assumed, the method of trading good and services. Gradually the idea of a 'unit currency' developed, at first using animal skins, salt and other items, until around 1,100 BC, the Chinese moved from the use of actual weapons and tools to trading in miniature replicas of weapons and tools. The expression 'promise to pay the bearer ...' started to take root, although it was soon realised that sharp and pointy miniature replicas were difficult to carry around (and were potentially lethal!), and so the flat coin of modern currency was developed.

In 600 BC, King Alyattes of Lydia minted the first official state currency. The coins were stamped with pictures that served as denominations for the coins and so in the city of Sardis, in about 600 BC, a clay pot might set you back an owl and a snake! At the same time as the Lydians were denominating coins, the Chinese were pulling ahead in the development of modern currency and were starting to print paper money. Where the US dollar now states 'In God We Trust', the Chinese emperor's money in the thirteenth century AD (when Marco Polo arrived in China) stated 'All Counterfeiters will be Decapitated'. Harsh, perhaps, but no doubt effective!

In contrast, Europeans continued to use coins until about 1,600 AD when, eventually, the banks started to print promissory notes to ease the transporting of large sums (although their value was based on the fact that bearers were entitled to exchange these notes at any point for gold and silver in the form of coins). However, unlike modern currency, these notes were issued by private banks and not by government, and therefore lacked the relative security of state backing. If the bank went bust, your paper promissory note was worth nothing and there was very little means of recourse ...

In the colonies of North and South America, difficulties in relying on transports between the Americas and Europe meant that bank notes were often short in supply. Therefore, the colonial governments improvised, printing 'IOU' notes that operated as money, and, in some cases, the governments were even more resourceful. In 1685 in Canada, at the time a French colony, the governor issued denominated and signed playing cards to serve as money, and the soldiers used these instead of relying on coins from France.

The increase in international trade meant that the stability of a particular government or monarchy affected the value of that country's currency and speculation on national currencies was in full effect by the seventeenth century. This was mainly in an attempt to increase the return on one's own country's goods (and thus increase national wealth), but also was used in efforts to weaken another country and reduce the threat their army or navy posed in a war.

Using another tactic, in the sixteenth century, Henry VIII of England famously set off an inflationary spiral by 'debasing' gold and silver coins with copper to pay for his wars. By reducing the value of gold or silver content relative to face value, governments extracted usable revenue from domestic money stocks. This strategy was called 'debasement' because each coin was worth less in terms of its precious metal content, and this event of the sixteenth century is called the 'Great Debasement'. Normally, the face value of the coined money exceeded its production cost, including the cost of the precious metals, and the difference between the production cost and the face value of the coin was earned by the King as profit. The Crown of England, like many governments, held an exclusive monopoly on the privilege to coin money from precious metals, and used the profits to help pay for government expenditures. This policy is effectively comparable to the modern strategy of 'quantitative easing' whereby the amount of money in circulation is increased in order to expand the funds available to pay for debts, make loans etc.

During the 'Great Debasement' the English crown's profits from debasement rose hugely. In March 1542 the value of the silver content of each English coin averaged 75% of each coin's face value. By March 1545 the value of the silver content had fallen to 50%, and by March 1546 to approximately 33%. The value of each coin in terms of its actual silver content had fallen to only 25% of face value by the time the debasement had run its course in 1551.

During a period of coinage debasement, a mechanism called 'Gresham's law' comes into play. Gresham's law is sometimes expressed as 'bad currency drives out good currency'. Households and businesses will hoard the good (or undebased) coinage, and use the debased coinage to pay for goods and services. The result is that only the debased currency remains in circulation, and the good currency goes into hiding or is spent on goods from foreign countries where the debased currency is not legal tender and therefore not acceptable.

In 1561 the English government under Queen Elizabeth I brought in a plan to retire the debased currency and replace it with currency the face value of which corresponded with its precious metal content. Retiring the debased currency was a tricky affair because, in accordance with Gresham's law, households and businesses tended to hoard good coinage and pay debts with debased coinage. In order to address this, the outflow of 'good' coinage to foreign markets was banned, and the use of the debased coinage was outlawed beyond a certain date. This is similar to when the Bank of England brings in a 'new' £20 note, for example, and a grace period is given for the use of the 'old' note, after which it is no longer valid currency.

Money is therefore essentially an abstract concept with practical applications, and nowhere more so than trading in stocks and shares, where the 'money' invested is only ever abstract. In stocks and shares, the perceived value of an asset is the only measure and, as a consequence, stocks and shares see many of the most extreme fluctuations.

At the beginning of the eighteenth century, the world witnessed the first 'stock exchange crash'. In the years after Jonathan Castaing began posting regular lists of stocks and commodity prices at Jonathan's Coffee House, and the London Stock Exchange effectively came into existence, there was a rush to invest in all manner of companies, particularly those trading in the Americas. At the height of this first boom, in 1720, there was an offer to invest in 'a company for carrying out an undertaking of great advantage, but nobody to know what it is'

… Unsurprisingly, the exchange was soon to crash as the perceived value of investment lowered with the realisation that returns from the Americas were not anywhere near as high as had been anticipated.

Similarly, the twentieth and twenty-first century stock market crashes show that 'money' is essentially about perceived confidence in the value of certain assets. Following the 1929 Wall Street Crash, whilst much of the world struggled, those whose wealth was invested in assets which were seen to retain their value did not suffer. Famously, John B. Kelly, father of Princess Grace of Monaco (formerly Grace Kelly), had never speculated on the stock exchange and the Kellys therefore enjoyed a life of genteel luxury during the 1930s and 1940s, with their money invested in cash and government bonds. In the same way, those whose 'money' was invested in such commodities or assets as oil and gold weathered the crashes of the 1980s and the early 2000s in relatively fine fettle, and in the UK, whilst there is often talk of a 'house price bubble' (which occasionally 'bursts'), ultimately, property has shown itself to be a place where our 'money' can be relatively safely stored.

So, in essence, then as now, 'money' is a concept based on a perception of value and is an expression of that value. The actual value of the paper on which money is printed is negligible and, whether it is Zimbabwean dollars in the twenty-first century or German Marks in the twentieth century, we may find ourselves at a point where the 'money' itself is worth less than its own weight in kindling paper. The UK property market is another case in point. How much is a house worth in the UK? It depends whether you're talking about London or Lincolnshire. It is, of course, not about the material value of the bricks and contents, but the perceived value of the asset, and how much people are prepared to pay (based upon, crucially, how much confidence they have in what they can ultimately sell it for!).

'Money' is, therefore, a psychological and sociological creation which gives the holder the power to purchase goods and services. And the possession of vast wealth puts us in a different position, psychologically and socially, to the majority of the population. The perception of the 'value' of money changes with its acquisition, in that our relationship to the process of exchanging goods is fundamentally changed through possession of enough wealth to no longer require us to know the price of bread, eggs, milk, a car, a house, an education, or any other commodity. These items cease to have any 'value' because we do not have to consider their worth, or lack of it – our ability to acquire them without a second thought means that they become psychologically insignificant and therefore 'meaningless' items, and the 'money' used to purchase them is also therefore meaningless. And so begins the process of detachment from the value of money which is part of the issue for people with wealth.

The Problem with Money

In a recent, highly publicised drink-driving trial in Texas, a sixteen-year-old boy claimed in his defence that his family's wealth should exempt him from responsibility for the deaths of four people. The boy, as many saw it, 'got off lightly' with ten years' probation and therapy (for which his family will pay privately), angering many with what they saw as the law's unfair leniency.[1]

Psychologist G. Dick Miller, who acted as an expert witness for the defence in the Texas case, argued that the boy was suffering from 'affluenza', which may have kept him from comprehending the full consequences of his actions. Although controversial, the essential argument put forward was that his wealthy background meant that he had not developed the social and psychological skills that we would usually expect a person of his age to possess – such as empathy and an awareness of consequences.

The term 'affluenza' is often dismissed as a silly buzzword created to express our cultural disdain for consumerism. However, although often used in jest, the term may have more truth than many of us would like to think and is perhaps comparable to the Great Debasement or a policy of quantitative easing whereby perceived value is reduced and any stable sense of 'worth' is directly affected.

Wealth, and the pursuit of it, has often been linked with immoral behaviour, and not just in recent films such as *The Wolf of Wall Street*. Psychologists who study the impact of wealth and inequality on humans have found that money can significantly influence our thoughts and behaviour in ways that we're often not aware of, no matter what our economic circumstances are. Although the concept of 'wealth' is certainly subjective, most of the current research measures wealth on scales of income, job status or measures of socioeconomic circumstances, like educational attainment and intergenerational wealth.

Several studies have sought to show that wealth may limit the development of empathy and compassion. Research published in the journal *Psychological Science* also found that, in general, people of lower economic status were instinctively better at reading others' facial expressions – an important marker of empathy – than wealthier people.[2]

The argument is that less wealthy individuals have to respond to a number of vulnerabilities and social threats that do not affect more wealthy individuals and, as such, they need to depend on others to tell them if a social threat or opportunity is coming. In essence, this makes them (through necessity) more perceptive of emotions than their wealthier counterparts.

This is perhaps similar to achieving fitness and strength through exercise – in order for muscles to grow and develop, we need an optimal level of resistance and pressure. Too much, and the muscle is overwhelmed. Too little and the muscle atrophies or, at best, fails to grow. In essence, the brain is no different and will develop in line with the challenges (or lack thereof) placed before it.[3]

Whether or not we wince at the findings of these studies, the basic point being made is that the possession of wealth affects not just our lifestyles, but also our psychological development and processes. It affects the way our brain's reward systems are established and, as such, having money can lead to as many costs as there are benefits to our happiness, our relationships and both our physical and emotional wellbeing.

The Inverted U-Shaped Curve

Malcolm Gladwell, author of a number of books on sociological issues such as *David and Goliath*, discusses the significance of the 'inverted U-shaped curve', or, in more mathematical language, the 'straightened bell-shaped curve', in consideration of a number of situations. He explores how the phenomenon of the inverted U-shaped curve can be seen with regard to crime and punishment and the 'three strikes' rule of the US legal system. He notices how, initially, the effect of harsher punishments does work to decrease crime rates. However, after a certain length of time, the effect levels out and crime levels do not respond to harsher punishments. As time passes again, the inconceivable occurs and harsher punishments actually cause an increase in crime levels. Gladwell explains this within the context of the ripple effect, in that incarcerating an individual affects not only that individual but their family and community. One example of a negative indirect 'ripple' effect is that persons whose parents are sent to jail suffer higher rates of psychological, social and educational problems, and thus the problems of one or two parents are passed to their children.

Similarly, Gladwell notices that in reducing class sizes in schools, we always assume that 'smaller is best'. However, research shows that the positive effect is most pronounced in the reduction to thirty students and there is a 'levelling off' of benefits when thirty is reduced to twenty. When the class becomes smaller than twenty, there is a negative effect on overall educational levels – there is almost too much individual attention and no learning to operate as part of a larger community, including the need to learn how to tolerate and work with differing opinions.

In terms of money, there is a comparable effect in that the link between wealth and increased wellbeing has a limit, following which there is a 'levelling off' of perceived benefit, and then, almost inconceivably, a decline in wellbeing beyond a certain point.

In 2010, a landmark Princeton University study showed that money can buy happiness – but only up to a very specific point. The researchers, including Nobel Prize-winning economist Daniel Kahneman, found that up to approximately a $75,000 annual income (around £50,000) closely correlates with increasing emotional wellbeing. Beyond that, however, more income doesn't translate into more happiness. Describing their findings, the authors wrote:

> Perhaps $75,000 is a threshold beyond which further increases in income no longer improve individuals' ability to do what matters most to their emotional well-being, such as spending time with people they like, avoiding pain and disease, and enjoying leisure.[4]

Using Gladwell's concept of the 'inverted U-shaped curve', it is not that after approximately £50,000 one becomes unhappy, but that after a bracket of approximately £50,000 to £75,000 ($75,000 to $100,000), the benefits of money in terms of wellbeing and happiness level off. At an income of approximately £50,000 to £75,000, most of our immediate needs are met and we can 'enjoy' the benefits of these – for example, holidays, housing and being able to consider a future which is free from the most pressing of anxieties. However, after a certain point on the straightened bell-shaped curve, the benefits actually decrease and the previous gains are lost as we become more detached from the 'value' of what we possess.

In 1890, the psychologist William James in his seminal work *The Principles of Psychology* noted that our achievements themselves matter far less than how we *perceive* those achievements. In athletic competitions there are clear winners and losers. In the Olympics, the gold medallists win the competition; the silver medallists have achieved slightly less, and the bronze medallists have managed a lower achievement still. We might, therefore, expect that happiness with their achievements would mirror this order, with the gold medallist being happiest, followed by the silver medallist, and then the bronze. If you assume that this is the case, it is worth watching the 2010 Vancouver Olympics medal ceremony for the women's moguls.[5] We surely expect that Jennifer Heil, having won the silver medal, would be happier than Shannon Bahrke, so why does it appear as if Bahrke is so much more pleased with her bronze medal than Heil is with her 'superior' silver?

This can be explained by what some psychologists call 'counterfactual thinking', which essentially means that our happiness with our achievements is usually measured against 'what might have been'. In other words, the silver medallist at the Olympics is often only thinking of how close they came to gold, whereas the bronze medallist considers an outcome where they won nothing! The comparison between being a medallist and winning nothing at all does not occur to the silver medallist. As such, when we are aware of what we have in comparison to having significantly less, we are happier than we are when we have plenty and are not able to employ 'counterfactual thinking' which focuses below where we are. Therefore, even though a person with an income of £75,000 per annum is objectively less well-off than a person with an income of £750,000, the person on £75,000, using the principle of counterfactual thinking, would be more pleased with their achievements (in comparison with having, for example, an income of £25,000, which is one third of their current level) than a person on £750,000 would be in comparison with a person who has an income of £250,000.

The possession of vast wealth seems to damage our ability to enjoy the simple things in life, which can then offset the happiness brought about by that wealth. Essentially, wealth can lead us to lose our 'savouring ability'. To demonstrate this, research subjects exposed to reminders of significant wealth (for example, a picture of large sums of money) were less able to enjoy a piece of chocolate that was given them to eat.[6] This is, at least in part, due to the psychological splitting of wealth and reward. Up to an income of approximately £50,000 to £75,000, if I work a certain number of hours a week for a specific salary (which I can work out in pounds per hour), there is a direct link between what I buy or how I spend my free time (for example, leisure and holidays) and my work. Without that link, it is hard to psychologically connect the two and the psychological understanding of reward is fundamentally altered. 'Money' takes on a new meaning – a less important one – and a process of 'debasement' occurs.

In Nick Hornby's *About a Boy*, one of the main characters, whose income comes from a famous Christmas song written by his father (which he despises), tries to get around this disconnection by dividing his day into units of half an hour.

> His way of coping with the days was to think of activities as units of time, each unit consisting of about thirty minutes. Whole hours, he found, were more intimidating, and most things one could do in a day took half an hour. Reading the paper, having a bath, tidying the flat, watching Home and Away and Countdown, doing a quick crossword on the toilet, eating breakfast and lunch, going to the local shops … That was nine units of a twenty-unit day (the evenings didn't count) filled by just the basic necessities. In fact, he had reached a stage where he wondered how his friends could juggle life and a job. Life took up so much time, so how could one work and, say, take a bath on the same day? He suspected that one or two people he knew were making some pretty unsavoury short cuts.

Wealth and Psychological Problems

The message here is that wealth can numb us to enjoying simple pleasures – and that this is merely one aspect of the wider impact upon our psychological development. It explains why problems such as addictions and thrill-seeking behaviours are so prevalent amongst wealthy people, and why motivation and emotional control are often issues amongst those who rely on family funds to provide their income where there is no direct relation between work, income and reward.

So while wealth itself doesn't cause addiction or substance abuse, wealth has been linked with a higher susceptibility to addiction problems. A number of studies have found that affluent children are more vulnerable than their less wealthy peers to substance abuse issues, potentially because of high pressure to achieve and isolation from parents,[7] along with developmental issues relating to their brains' reward systems. These studies also found that these children may be more likely to internalise problems, which has been linked with substance abuse.[8] And it is not just adolescents; even in adulthood, the wealthy outdrink the poor by more than 27%.[9]

Children growing up in wealthy families may seem to have it all, but having it all may come at a high cost. Wealthier children tend to be more distressed than their lower-income peers and are at higher risk of anxiety, depression, substance abuse, eating disorders, cheating and stealing.[10]

This is a real issue where resolution is not straightforward but is linked to developmental psychological problems which can be addressed and improved with the right interventions. Essentially, intervention should be structured to restart developmental neurological and psychological processes which have been arrested.

One way to explain this is to consider Maslow's hierarchy of needs,[11] where the fundamental ingredients to optimise human development are set out.

Maslow's hierarchy of needs is based on the concept that we have a set of needs as human beings, which become increasingly sophisticated as the needs on the levels below are met. The most basic level of need is, of course, that of survival, with food, water, being able to regulate our temperatures and other primary requirements for the body to continue living. Unless these needs are met, the ones above are effectively irrelevant and, arguably, if these basic physiological needs are not being met, our attention will be focused on these above the others. The next level up is that of physical safety – to be able to live in an environment which is free from physical threat and where we can be secure enough to aspire to the next level: that of friendship, family and building relationships with others. Once we have achieved a relative degree of security on this level, Maslow argues that we are free to consider more abstract or higher-level needs – those of self-esteem, and finally of self-fulfilment.

Of course, within Maslow's hierarchy, for the upper-level needs to be achievable, the lower-level needs must be met. We are used to the concept that people who struggle to achieve the lower levels of need, due to poverty, war, displacement or illness, will subsequently struggle to achieve the upper levels of self-actualisation or self-esteem. However, what is also the case is that for those whose 'starting point' assumes absolutely that the bottom two needs (physiological and safety needs) are met, achieving the upper three levels (belonging/love, self-esteem and self-actualisation) is no less problematic.

As an analogy, if I am naturally right-handed, I will use my right hand more and therefore the dominance of that hand and the muscle strength and responsiveness of that side of my body will further develop. Children may be naturally right- or left-handed, but the fine and gross motor skills which develop mainly on one side are also due to a 'favouring' of that side, enabling its progression.

So it is with wealthy children and Maslow's hierarchy of needs. Children (who become adolescents and adults) who identify themselves as wealthy and are encouraged to do so by parents and other influential figures around them, children for whom wealth contributes significantly to their sense of self and then who, crucially, come to use it as the means to achieve rewards sought, are essentially 'favouring' this aspect above others. Just as I may struggle to use a pair of scissors with my left hand, so the adolescent and adult children of wealthy parents will struggle to use their other resources, having naturally come to rely on their wealth as a means to achieve reward. Other aspects of their psychological development (e.g. empathy and a sense of consequence, as discussed above) have been underused, and so the adolescent or adult lacks the skills and confidence (such as in their own resilience and self-reliance) which are essential to allowing them to progress through Maslow's hierarchy.

The children and especially the grandchildren of ultra-wealthy families do not go through the developmental stages needed to meet the challenges they are to face and to develop and establish their own sense of motivation and reward. When we consider this problem, we can think of examples such as the Vanderbilts and others who clearly did not progress through the stages of neurological and psychological growth that would have enabled them to make a link between action and consequence, or to think about the longer term.

The possession of wealth therefore brings significant personal and psychological challenges. It is essential to recognise the impact of wealth on our ambitions, skills, motivation and sense of self, and even on our neurological structures. If I have a level of wealth which is surplus to daily need, I will gradually become detached from the processes of exchange which are inherent to society. I will use my ample resources to purchase items, because I can easily – but the ease with which I can do so will 'debase' the exchange and change my perception of its worth and potentially the worth of both myself and others.

Having significant wealth unavoidably alters our percept of value and our psychological and sociological relationship with money and commodities. In a nutshell, it is a frequent source of difficulty for a child raised with a trust fund paying them £200,000 per annum from the age of eighteen or twenty-one to then take a graduate internship which pays £35,000 a year for a rigorous forty-hour week. That is a fundamental disruption in the individual's internal unit of value, and success in such an internship would require a total re-evaluation by the individual of their relationship to money and worth.

Therefore, if the aim is to avoid the three-generation wealth cycle (see following chapter), then acknowledgement of the psychology of wealth and its impact, accompanied by structured interventions which can help to address the negative aspects, is essential.

Summary and Suggested Tasks

In order to set up our children and grandchildren to be able to manage the opportunities that come their way, we need to help them to develop the key concepts of ownership, responsibility and, crucially, delayed gratification. Being able to delay gratification is the single most important factor in helping individuals to avoid addiction, appreciate the consequences of their actions and postpone pleasurable activities until they have achieved their set goals. How to do this is often difficult, particularly for parents who have the means to say 'yes' to most requests. Where our children are concerned, it can often feel as if providing in the short term (giving in to the demands) is easier to achieve than preparing our children for the long term and, in the process, subjecting them to a series of potentially difficult or emotionally challenging situations. But we argue that these difficult or emotionally challenging situations are developmentally essential and allow the child to grow resilience and emotional tolerance towards frustration, disappointment and sacrifice.

A straightforward task which can be done by all, and which starts to enable the skills set out above, is as follows. For those of you with a child or grandchild under twelve, open a bank account for that child and encourage them to have saving goals based on a set, and small, amount of pocket money per week or month. These should be initially small goals that gradually increase with age and should be to fund rewards and treats that they want or have asked for. These rewards and treats will be funded by them, not by you, and may be particularly desired and fashionable clothes, music, games, consoles, toys or anything else which they want and which you would usually provide without hesitation. From now on, try to avoid providing these items for your child and instead encourage them to save their money in their own account. And don't make it too easy! For example, a six-year-old child can be taught to wait for at least two to three weeks before they can afford to buy the teddy, game or book that they want. A twelve-year-old can wait at least a month to six weeks – they may not like it, but if you support them to do this, they will learn that they can delay their gratification and, crucially, can take ownership over the process of buying, the items themselves and the money with which they bought them. And they will likely take better care of these items than they would the ones they have been bought on a whim. Encouraging them to wait helps to develop an awareness of value, to build the ability to delay gratification, and to establish reward pathways around planning and achieving goals.

Chapter 3 – A quick reference guide:

1. Our attitude to money and what we think it 'is' will shape how we respond to it – how successfully we plan, how we are motivated by it (or not) and how we understand its value in terms of what it gives us.

2. Amongst second and particularly third generations, there can be significant psychological and neurological consequences of growing up without having to make decisions and choices based on limited resources. The brain doesn't naturally get the 'resistance' which helps build the pathways necessary to inspire motivation, ambition, striving and effective decision-making.

3. Understanding these principles is key to structuring interventions that will challenge individuals in the right ways to help them develop the underlying structures and skills they need to cope with the benefits and challenges of significant wealth.

Notes and References: Chapter 3

[1] Hennessy-Fiske, M., and Muskal, M. (2013) '"Affluenza" in Texas incites anger, lawsuits and call for jail time'. *Los Angeles Times*, December 19th. http://www.latimes.com/nation/nationnow/la-na-nn-affluenza-anger-lawsuits-jail-time-texas-20131219-story.html.

[2] Szalavitz, M. (2010) 'The Rich Are Different: More Money, Less Empathy'. *Time*, November 24th. http://healthland.time.com/2010/11/24/the-rich-are-different-more-money-less-empathy.

[3] Bergland, C. (2015) 'The Neuroscience of Making a Decision'. *Psychology Today*, May 6th.

[4] Sample, I (2010) 'The Price of Happiness? £50,000pa'. *Guardian*, September 6th. http://www.theguardian.com/science/2010/sep/06/earnings-pay-happiness-research.

[5] Available on YouTube: http://www.youtube.com/watch?v=oZrwczciJxo

[6] Quoidbach, J., et al. (2010) 'Money giveth, money taketh away: The dual effect of wealth on happiness'. *Psychological Science* 21, 759–763.

[7] Luthar, S.S. (2003) 'The Culture of Affluence: Psychological Costs of Material Wealth'. *Child Development* 74(6), 1581–1593. http://www.ncbi.nlm.nih.gov/pmc/articles/PMC1950124/.

[8] Ibid.

[9] Rufus, A. (2010) 'Who Drinks the Most Alcohol?' *Daily Beast*, December 29th. http://www.thedailybeast.com/articles/2010/12/29/drinking-stats-who-drinks-the-most-alcohol.html.

[10] Luthar, S.S. (2003).

[11] Maslow, A. (1954) *Motivation and Personality*. New York: Harper Press.

CHAPTER 4

The Problems with Wealth Transfer

Hans Kristian 'Tetra Pak' Rausing's very public struggle with addiction is an extreme but all too common example of many of the difficulties experienced by the successive generations of wealthy families. It also, arguably, epitomises some of the issues surrounding the psychology of money which we set out in Chapter 3.

Hans Rausing is reported to have struggled to find his own direction in life and his father's former assistant remembers how he was always in the 'shadow of his father'.[1] Famously, in 2012, after years of struggle with addiction, he was arrested for possession of Class-A drugs and his wife, Eva, was found dead at their home. As widely reported, he was given a suspended sentence for preventing the lawful burial of her body which had lain at their home for up to two months, a fact that testifies to the fragility of Hans Rausing's psychological state.

Hans Rausing is a dramatic and very public example, but one that underlines the reality that the context in which second- and third-generation wealthy are brought up is fundamentally different from that of the first generation and they cannot be expected to have the same motivations, ambitions or perceived need to develop their abilities as the first generation did. We can criticise them for it, we can shake our heads, talk of 'trust fund kids' disparagingly and wonder why they cannot achieve to the same level as their famous parents or grandparents – or we can understand the context in which the problems arise and deal with them.

Another high-profile example is that of the Vanderbilts, who exemplify the 'rags to riches and back again in three generations' mythology. What this family show is that there really is no limit to what a family can spend within a quarter of a century! Living descendants of the family have authored books with titles such as *Fortune's Children: The Fall of the House of Vanderbilt* and *Dead End Gene Pool* about the family's lost wealth. According to these accounts, there was virtually no structure or organisation in how the family transferred wealth from one generation to the next. Combined with this lack of structure and organisation was the fact that by the third decade of the twentieth century, the Vanderbilts had gone from being producers of vast wealth to consumers of it. The majority of the family members had no motivation to produce wealth and instead they spent it on luxury items, activities and fabulous parties, or gave it away to fashionable philanthropic causes. They had become, as some term it, the 'patsy rich' who were in essence the owners of 'dumb money' – 'dumb' because they had no idea what to do with it, how to use it constructively and to enhance their lives in a meaningful way, not just for the short term but for the duration. And the fact that this happened within a few generations shows how important the issue of our developmental progress is. The generations subsequent to Cornelius and William Vanderbilt had no 'resistance' to their neurological development, no checks on their choices and no way to build a grounded and meaningful relationship with wealth or with themselves as individuals and as a family system.

In considering the issues surrounding wealth and the transfer of wealth between generations, some key questions arise. This chapter sets out these concerns and explains how they are embedded in our attitudes to wealth, in how we interact with it and in the changes to our psychological development which wealth creates. The questions 'what is wealth?' and 'what is the purpose of wealth?' are fundamental to an understanding of how we respond to money and the opportunities, or challenges, it presents.

Within this are generational issues, as we go on to set out in Chapter 6, and the need to understand that the skills, needs, drives and motivations of one generation will almost certainly not be the same as for successive generations. The old Chinese proverb states that 'wealth does not sustain beyond three generations' and numerous examples in history testify to the truth of this proverb. Specifically, 'the pattern for family wealth seems fixed ... the first generation builds wealth and the second generation shepherds or preserves it. The third and succeeding generations spend it until it is dissipated.'[2] Although we can name individual families where this has not happened, they are only an exception to an almost universal rule. However, crucially, this shows that the three-generational cycle is avoidable.

Most approaches to wealth planning and management tend to focus on the mechanics, whereas the 'real, enduring wealth of a family is not financial capital. More important assets to sustaining the family's long term financial security are intellectual capital and human capital.'[3]

In this chapter, we discuss the underlying issues inherent in possessing and transferring wealth and how to address the 'rags to riches to rags in three generations' question through setting out the three main models of wealth transition management and planning, considering the pros and cons of each.

A thorny issue for any person who has wealth and is considering how, and whether, to pass that on to successive generations, is the question of entitlement. The entitlement issue is essentially the question of whether a potential receiver of the wealth is 'due' that inheritance as a matter of right. How does a child grow up with great wealth but without that sense of entitlement or, alternatively, a sense of resentment? Should they be passed that wealth (in its entirety), and what are the implications for family relationships of choosing not to pass it on?

The motivations and drives for first-generation wealth creators are almost always, though not without exception, based on an essential combination of need and ability. As Malcolm Gladwell sets out in *David and Goliath*,[4] for most people, ambition and motivation to succeed are rooted in a starting position of perceived inferiority (and thus arguably with little to lose). Entrepreneurial spirit, which often underlies wealth creation, is therefore more often found in the proverbial 'underdog' who has aspirations which drive him forward and a tangible sense of the potentially life-changing rewards. Along with this, the underdog has developed the psychological skills needed to progress and he is neurologically best-placed due to the challenges which have 'trained' his brain to work optimally.

For any successful first-generation wealth creators, however, the consequences for their children are that these offspring grow up in an environment which often bears little or no resemblance to the background of their parents. Schooling, housing, holidays and social environments – essentially every aspect of their lives – are often miles away from those of the first generation, although the significant wealth creation may arise at a point where the second generation still recall the early years before wealth (and have therefore been shaped by those years to some degree).

The second generation are, in practice, no longer the 'underdog' that their parents were and their needs and aspirations (along with their skills and abilities) will of course be different to those of the first generation. They are perhaps motivated by a different kind of insecurity to that of the first generation, for they, unlike their parents, do not have 'nothing to lose'. The risks of failure are therefore different. At the same time, they have perceptibly less to gain, and thus the second generation are seen as the 'preservers' of wealth – but where is the reward in that? They are not achieving for themselves, simply preventing loss – which is a different psychological and neurological experience for us to undergo.

And so, as the third and fourth generations come into existence, the link to the motivations and drives of the first generation becomes more indirect. Their brains' mechanisms as to how we experience a sense of satisfaction and reward are fundamentally altered. The third and fourth generations have no memory of being 'without', and their priorities, along with their answers to the questions 'what is wealth?' and 'what is the purpose of wealth?', will inevitably have shifted significantly.

The key to successful wealth transfer and planning is, therefore, understanding the issues facing each individual generation, where their motivations are and what their likely psychological and neurological developmental needs are. As Hans Kristian Rausing's father's former assistant described it, 'Hans Kristian had no need to work. He had everything. I had always dreamed of having an E-type Jaguar. And I remember the day he just rolled up in his E-type. Then he had a Ferrari. I'm still paying for my bloody Volvo!'[5]

The key drivers of 'need' and a tangible link between achievement and reward which existed for Hans Kristian Rausing's grandfather clearly no longer applied to the grandson, so why would we be surprised when Hans Kristian lacks the drive, ambition and discipline necessary to follow in his grandfather's (and father's) footsteps?

Key to this is not that money inevitably ruins the lives of successive generations, but that what is crucial in first and successive generations of wealthy people is the development of emotional intelligence (EQ).[6] Specifically, the more EQ a person has, the more psychologically developed they are, the more they can use their wealth in a healthy and constructive way. For wealthy individuals and their children, the pressures and the lack of normal social limits or 'need'-driven motivational ambitions make the development of EQ of particular relevance.

As Gladwell describes, there is a tipping point where there is 'too much' wealth, but how much that is varies from individual to individual. One frequently positive arrangement, however, is where children have a basic set of financial fall-backs meaning that a failed risk would not cause total ruin, but a successful risk would still yield meaningful rewards. This is where 'entrepreneurial spirit' exists and the 'underdog' flourishes.

At both extremes of wealth (both having and being without) there is an unusual relationship with risk and consequence. At the one extreme, to take even small risks might mean homelessness or starvation, whilst at the other, there is often a sense of entitlement, rather than struggle, and an existence which is divorced from reality and where there are no real, tangible and life-changing consequences – either good or bad – of any actions.

A client of ours, Peter, who was approaching thirty and had been recently promoted to a senior management position within a large multinational company (into which he had been headhunted due to the success of his own business which he had established at the age of twenty-three), described his motivators and his insecurities. He recalled how, for periods of time during his childhood, dinner was 'bread with no butter and breakfast was cornflakes with water as we couldn't afford milk'. He said that he had decided, as a child, that he would 'never, ever live like this again' and had committed himself from the age of eleven to doing all that was necessary to raise himself out of poverty. This involved significant personal sacrifices, particularly during school when he eschewed most social contact at his large state school in order to avoid 'getting distracted' – but the rewards were tangible.

Now, as an adult, he described how he was 'starting to get more nervous' and that sometimes he felt himself less able to just 'go for it'. He was aware that he now had a lot more to lose than he did just a few years before. He said that, in a way, being David was emotionally easier than being Goliath as it wasn't 'such a long way down'.

Evolutionarily, humans are designed to take risks only where the assessed reward is at least adequate. Where there is neither risk nor tangible reward, it is necessary to find other motivations, otherwise the natural human tendency is to remain static. For second- and third-generation wealth inheritors, and their descendants, this is where EQ becomes essential. Issues of self-esteem, self-worth and self-awareness play a vital part in providing motivators which are perhaps more abstract than those of the first-generation wealth creators, but no less important.

Three Models of Wealth Transfer

'The Warren Buffett Model' – The Family Inherit Nothing

In a recent interview,[7] the singer and former Police frontman Sting stated that in relation to the passing of his estimated £180m wealth to his children, 'I certainly don't want to leave them trust funds that are albatrosses around their necks. They have to work. All my kids know that and they rarely ask me for anything, which I really respect and appreciate.'

He went on to say, 'Obviously, if they were in trouble, I would help them, but I've never really had to do that.'[8] He added that 'they have this work ethic that makes them want to succeed on their own merit' and he is 'enormously proud of that'.

TV personality and chef Nigella Lawson, daughter of a former Chancellor of the Exchequer, agreed with Sting's position when she publicly stated, 'I am determined my children should have no financial security. It ruins people not having to earn money.'[9]

Sting and Nigella Lawson can be seen as proponents of the 'Warren Buffett' model of wealth transfer – in essence, the family inherit nothing. This can be roughly translated as an approach which aims to give children a springboard to success, through education and by letting them know they have a fall-back if they are in serious trouble, but beyond that, the philosophy is one which believes that how they live should depend on their own personal achievements and not those of others. It is an approach which is designed not to punish or withhold, but to inspire ambition and a motivation to succeed through individual merit, with the self-esteem and psychological development which comes through having to exert oneself in pursuit of a personal goal – whatever that might be. It is also an approach which emphasises the link between work and reward, something which of course might be expected from the son of a former dock worker (Sting) and the daughter of a financial expert (Lawson)!

Warren Buffett has pledged to give away 99% of his wealth, either during his life or on his death, with 83% pledged to the Gates Foundation.[10] The Buffett model, and how it is described by those who adhere to it, may seem odd to many who might struggle to understand why a person would work all their life, simply to pass it to a foundation on death rather than to members of their family – but it is an approach which is indicative of a high level of EQ and an ability to set clear and purposeful boundaries for future generations.

In an even more extreme variant of the Buffett model (although perhaps to be taken slightly tongue-in-cheek), Mayor of New York City Michael Bloomberg once famously stated that 'the best financial planning ends with bouncing the check to the undertaker'.[11] Like Buffett, Bloomberg intends for his children to have every opportunity, but any success or wealth will be theirs and theirs alone, rather than given to them by their father. Bloomberg intends that his children not be demotivated by what Sting calls the 'albatross of wealth'.

The reasons for pursuing a non-inheritance policy with regard to the next generation can vary from a genuine desire to see children succeed on their own merits and a belief that they have the skills and ability (Sting, Bloomberg and Buffett) to a strongly held belief, as expressed by Nigella Lawson, that inherited wealth can be enormously damaging. In a very different example, such a policy can also be, as in the case of Gina Rinehart, Australia's wealthiest woman, due to a total lack of faith in the skills and personal character of the next generations. Gina Rinehart is on record (filed in court documents) as claiming that 'None of the plaintiffs [her children] has the requisite capacity or skill, nor the knowledge, experience, judgement or responsible work ethic to administer a trust ... as part of the growing HPPL Group'.[12]

Whatever the reasons for implementing the Buffett model, the non-inheritance policy has significant familial and social implications, with the majority of wealth passed from those such as Warren Buffett, Michael Bloomberg, and Pierre and Pam Omidyar reaching charitable and philanthropic causes. Such efforts are targeted and intended to achieve the maximum benefit for as significant a number of people as possible. The intention is not to create a dynasty, but to leave a legacy.

The reality for the children of those who follow this policy of wealth transfer is that whilst their childhoods may be entirely provided for, their adulthood is their own responsibility (albeit with connections and networks available to them that others may only dream of). The risk of this approach is that some may fail to achieve financial or personal success, but the Buffett approach is almost Darwinian in its outlook and understands that need often drives success. Without need, where is the motivation to succeed? We would perhaps add that without need, the necessary preconditions for success in terms of psychological and neurological development do not exist.

It is an approach which parents may find hard to contemplate, with fears of being considered 'selfish' or 'cold' towards their own children an emotional hurdle for those lacking in EQ. And this is therefore where the EQ of the parent and their encouragement of the development of EQ in their children is key. To say 'no' for the good of the child is a basic parenting skill that we can all understand. But where the 'no' in question flies in the face of the way the majority of the world's population live – accumulating as much as possible during their lifetime and then leaving all they can to their children – it can be particularly difficult for both generations involved.

'The Bill Gates Model' – The Family Inherit Some ... but Not All

Bill Gates has come out in favour of a second model of wealth transfer in relation to his children, where he will 'give the kids some money but not a meaningful percentage'.[13] His goal is to set the number 'so that they need to work but they feel reasonably taken care of'.[14]

However, Mr Gates has acknowledged the challenge of this model: the specific amount for his goal is 'hard to figure out' and the question of need versus surplus is difficult to assess accurately. Bill Gates is effectively trying to answer the question of 'at what point does inheritance change from being supportive to being a demotivating "albatross"?'

In a recent interview, Gates stated, 'I knew I didn't think it was a good idea to give the money to my kids. That wouldn't be good either for my kids or society,'[15] and yet his desire is to leave them with a relatively significant amount, to ensure their basic future needs are met.

For both Gates and Buffett, the assumption is that total possession of family wealth for the benefit of one family alone is unhealthy and undesirable. Their position is based on an assumption in part of social responsibility but also, importantly, of parental responsibility. For Bill Gates, providing for every material need that his children may have as adults will ensure that they never want for anything, and yet, at the same time, what is at risk of being taken away – their sense of independence, of self-worth, of motivation and of personal achievement – is of far more value.

For the Gates model, and those considering it for their own families, the discussion again relates to the questions 'what is wealth?' and 'what is the purpose of wealth?' The point at which one becomes 'wealthy' is key for the Gates model, and of course this is always related both to the individuals involved and the cultural context in which those individuals live, and to the reasons for which the wealth in question is being passed. It is a complex process and one which should be considered as such.

'The Carlos Slim Model' – The Family Inherit Everything

The third, perhaps most traditional, model of wealth transfer is one where the majority of the wealth is kept within the family. In this approach, the efforts of the family are to preserve that wealth and pass it to future generations.

It is this approach to wealth transfer which has been publicly supported by Carlos Slim Helú,[16] who was, in 2013, listed by Forbes as the world's second richest man and who, by transferring his inheritance to his descendants during his lifetime, is attempting to avoid potential infighting among his descendants.

Slim has been quoted as saying that it's more important to leave his children with the responsibility of managing a company than with a pile of cash. According to Grupo Carso's 2012 report filed with Mexico's Bolsa, sons Carlos, Patrick and Marco Antonio Slim Domit each own, directly or indirectly, more than 10% of Grupo Carso. Slim Helú and daughters Soumaya, Vanessa and Johanna also own an equal percentage. In addition, the seven jointly possess 10% of the shares in the trust run by Inbursa and InCarso. Added together, the report shows that the family control 79.61% of Grupo Carso, a global conglomerate. Carlos Slim Helú, a Catholic whose wife died in 1999, is a strong believer in family values and is known to stay very close to his family.

Importantly, Carlos Slim's cultural background and its resulting effect on his neurological structures and sense of reward must be taken into account. His family continue to be based in a country where there are extremes of wealth and poverty, with the risks of poverty (or even relative poverty) high – and the cultural context is therefore very different to that of Bloomberg's New York. The closeness of the family unit is also relevant and Carlos Slim's businesses remain in the control of his immediate family, operating for the benefit of the family. Philanthropy and the considerations of society as a whole, such as concern Bill Gates, take a less prioritised position within the 'Slim' model – although this is not to say that a great deal of good is not done by the philanthropic work carried out by the family.

There are a number of families who show that the Slim model of family inheritance is by no means one which is doomed to a three-generational rags-riches-rags fate of creation and loss. The Rothschilds are a high-profile example of a family where wealth was successfully secured, passed and built upon for numerous generations. Although now, in the early twenty-first century, nowhere near as significant as in the nineteenth century, the fact remains that the Rothschilds' name, and wealth, is still substantial.

However, what the Rothschilds were able to do for almost 200 years and what the Slim family have done more recently is dependent on significant contributions from skilled and able members of the family within each generation. To an extent, what the Rothschilds show about the Slim model is that, in the long term, to succeed over multiple generations, the 'first generation' will, in effect, start all over again. This phenomenon of the 'phases' of the family office is discussed in chapters 1 and 6. It is clear that any attempt to preserve wealth within a family which grows in number, and often grows apart in terms of relationships, will require an understanding of the 'phases' of how the structure develops.

What Will Be Right for Your Family?

To be able to answer this question is key to being able to plan for the future and to prepare future generations for whichever option is the family's preferred choice. At this point, it is important that you sit down as a family where this is possible, and talk through your values, your vision for your children and grandchildren, and how you want the money to be used. It is impossible to make a decision about what you want to happen unless you are clear why. The arguments for each method are valid, and each method has its benefits and its potential downsides.

To be clear about the family's vision for wealth transfer is essential in order to plan and educate the family as to what is going to happen, so that they can prepare themselves. In the examples listed above, the plans are clear, have been set out well in advance of any potential handover of control between generations and, importantly, are known to the family. It is easy to imagine that Warren Buffet's children may feel resentful (and this may, of course, be the case). However, it seems that through planning, preparation and education, the reasons for the lack of inheritance and the passing of minimal wealth between generations have been both philosophically and practically set out, and all individuals concerned have had time to prepare, both emotionally and psychologically – but also, crucially, they will have been neurologically wired to anticipate this.

Summary

There is, crucially, no objective right or wrong in how to approach the question of wealth transfer. The culture of the individual family and the realities of effective succession (depending on the skills and abilities of future generations) are key. Fundamental to any of these three approaches, however, is the development of EQ, which will enable families either to prepare future generations for non-inheritance or to ensure, where the Slim model is favoured, that successive generations are ready, intellectually, practically, emotionally, psychologically and ethically, for the challenges they face.

Chapter 4 – A quick reference guide:

1. Ask, 'What is the culture of my family?' and compare this with other members of the family to ensure you are in agreement. Do you see the passing of wealth as a gift or an albatross around the necks of future generations? Do you want to give the gift of money, or the gift of responsibility?

2. Write a list where you think about what the skills and abilities of the individuals in successive generations are and what they need to be able to do – and what skills and abilities can be developed.

3. There is no 'right' or 'wrong' with regard to wealth transfer – the only 'wrong' is a lack of planning and a lack of clarity. Successful wealth transfer requires planning, preparation and setting of specific and achievable expectations.

Notes and References: Chapter 4

[1] Bezant quoted by Bingham (2012) 'Eva Rausing death: dogged by drugs until the very end'. *Telegraph*, August 1st. http://www.telegraph.co.uk/news/uknews/crime/9443706/Eva-Rausing-death-dogged-by-drugs-until-the-very-end.html.

[2] Carlson, R. (2009) 'Avoiding Rags to Riches to Rags'. InvestorsInsight, June 11th. http://www.investorsinsight.com/blogs/retirement_watch/archive/2009/06/11/avoiding-rags-to-riches-to-rags.aspx.

[3] Ibid.

[4] Gladwell, M (2014) *David and Goliath: Underdogs, Misfits and the Art of Battling Giants*. New York: Little, Brown and Company.

[5] Bezant quoted by Bingham (2012).

[6] There are three models of EQ in current thinking. The ability model, developed by Salovey, Mayer and Caruso in 2004 ('Emotional Intelligence: Theory, Findings and Implications', *Psychological Inquiry* 15(3), 197–215), focuses on the individual's ability to process emotional information and use it to navigate social environments. The trait model, as

developed by Petrides and Furnham in 2001 ('Trait Emotional Intelligence: Psychometric Investigation with Reference to Established Trait Taxonomies', *European Journal of Personality* 15(6), 425–448), encompasses both behavioural dispositions and self-perception of abilities and it is measured through self-report. The final model, the mixed model, is a combination of both ability and trait EQ. The mixed-model approach to EQ defines it as an array of skills and characteristics that drive leadership performance, as proposed by Daniel Goleman in 1998 ('What Makes a Leader?', *Harvard Business Review* 76(6), 93–102).

While arguments abound as to what constitutes 'EQ', studies have shown that people with high EQ as measured using various scales and testing tools possess greater mental health, exemplary job performance and more potent leadership skills.

[7] Grieg, G. (2014) 'Why my children will not be inheriting my £180million fortune'. *Mail on Sunday*, June 22nd. http://www.dailymail.co.uk/home/event/article-2662557/.

[8] Ibid.

[9] Ibid.

[10] Willett (2013) '15 Tycoons Who Won't Leave Their Fortunes To Their Kids'. Business Insider, August 20th. http://www.businessinsider.com/tycoons-not-leaving-money-to-their-kids-2013-8.

[11] Ibid.

[12] Ibid.

[13] *Deccan Herald* (2014) 'Bill Gates "will not leave a fortune for his children"'. September 20th. http://www.deccanherald.com/content/98105/bill-gates-not-leave-fortune.html.

[14] Ibid.

[15] Ibid.

[16] Estevez, D. (2013) 'Mexican Billionaire Carlos Slim is quietly transferring assets to his children'. Forbes, November 19th. http://www.forbes.com/sites/doliaestevez/2013/11/19/mexican-billionaire-carlos-slim-is-quietly-transferring-assets-to-his-children/.

CHAPTER 5

Integral Consulting and Ken Wilber

This chapter is designed to be an 'optional' read and it is possible (and perfectly permissible!) to jump forward to Chapter 6 if you wish to at this point. Although we base our approach in a range of different theories and research from some of the world's most advanced thinkers, we recognise that a more in-depth understanding of the philosophical principles which lie behind our model is not necessarily of interest for all! This chapter is provided for those who wish to know more about our theoretical and research-based underpinnings, but is not designed to put off readers whose interests do not extend into this area. Therefore, please read on if this is of interest to you, but if not, then feel free to jump forward to Chapter 6, which can be read and understood without needing to reference the ideas raised in this chapter.

This chapter provides an overview of the philosophical and research-based principles behind our innovative strategy for the establishment, organisation and management of our clients' family businesses and offices, the search for investment opportunities, the screening of these opportunities and their ultimate selection or rejection. These principles are grounded in the philosophies of Ken Wilber, whose understanding of how humans develop relationally and psychologically, and of how this both reflects and is mirrored in the health of the external structures which surround them, is key to understanding how to establish and maintain successful family wealth management systems.

Integral Investing

Our approach to the management of our clients' family offices draws on the most advanced thinking in international finance, economics, psychology and philosophy. This approach, as mentioned, is one which is grounded in the philosophies of Ken Wilber,[1] who argues that in order to maximise success, health and stability and to achieve our potential – either as organisations or as individuals – we must consider all aspects of both our internal and external worlds, and how these aspects interlink and inform the development of the other aspects. Wilber's worldview has been termed 'a theory of everything', and it is this unparalleled approach to knowledge which informs us in all our dealings. According to Jack Crittenden, Ph.D.,[2] 'the twenty-first century literally has three choices: Aristotle, Nietzsche, or Ken Wilber'. We have chosen Wilber.

The relevance of Ken Wilber to business and wealth management is something which has been noted and discussed for over a decade, particularly since the publication of his *A Theory of Everything* in 2001. Writers and business analysts have considered the applicability of Wilber's ideas, and the potential of this approach has been of interest in terms of the 'map' which these ideas appear to provide for successful business and financial systems and management.[3]

Integral Investing is a cutting-edge investment model based on Wilber's Integral Theory that targets both premium financial market and premium impact returns for the benefit of all. It allows the integration of traditional financial due diligence alongside environmental, social, and governance criteria, as well as including tools for the measurement and development of the operational and potential levels of culture, behaviour and consciousness of the organisation and individuals within it.

Wilber's integral approach is essentially the coherent organisation, coordination, and harmonisation of all of the relevant practices, understandings, methodologies and experiences available to human beings. We therefore start here by setting out an introduction to Wilber's theory in a general sense, before outlining the relevance and applicability of this theory to business and, in particular, the management of family offices.

Integral Investing and Ken Wilber's 'Theory of Everything'

In order to understand the relevance of Ken Wilber's philosophy to the organisation, structuring and management of family offices, it is important first to set out his theories in terms of the fundamental understandings of the systems and structures of our internal and external worlds, of our individual and collective realities, which are developed.

Wilber's approach is to define the different aspects of our internal and external worlds into four quadrants and, within these quadrants, to consider the level of development achieved. This approach is termed 'All Quadrants, All Levels' (AQAL) in that no aspect of our existence is outside the schema and all are relevant to the success of any endeavour, whether personal or professional.

Wilber noted how previous philosophers, theorists and thinkers tended to focus on one aspect of our existence and thus, whilst important, their contributions can only be partial in terms of the overall understanding of our individual and collective reality.

The appeal of Ken Wilber is in his ability to provide a uniquely sensible and applicable framework to the myriad of thought systems, knowledge and understandings that have developed throughout history. The key word here is 'developed' in that Wilber's theory sets out how human knowledge has evolved and he reintroduces to a post-modern world the argument that there is a hierarchy in our systems of understanding – there is such a thing as advancement and it is no longer a case of 'everybody has won, and all must have prizes' (to quote Lewis Carroll in *Alice's Adventures in Wonderland*).

At the same time, Wilber's system does not propose one system of thinking – for example, a post-enlightenment Western egocentric philosophy – at the expense of another. Whilst fundamentally hierarchical, Wilber's construction is essentially 'holarchical', including rather than excluding previous systems and understandings. And within this, Wilber leaves room for his theory to be further developed – it is '*a* theory', not '*the* theory of everything'.

The Four-Quadrant Model – All Quadrants, All Levels (AQAL)

The Upper Quadrants – The Individual Internal and External

Wilber argues that our reality can be divided into four interrelated but distinct quadrants. The aspects of our reality are categorised as Upper Left ('I'), Upper Right ('It'), Lower Left ('We') and Lower Right ('Its').

The Upper Left quadrant is designated as indicating the relative development of the individual internally, the 'subjective' or 'internal' individual. This is the 'I' of human consciousness and is the seat of individual motivations, internal subjective emotional development, individual desires and intellectual advancement.

The Upper Left quadrant considers the thought process and reality from the perspective of the individual who is experiencing it. It might include imagery, internal vocalisation, a remembered taste, smell or image of previous experiences, or a set of emotional interpretations of the meaning of a thought. This is the conscious experience of the individual person who is thinking the thought. It is internal to the person, and cannot be known unless the person chooses to share their internal experience through some means of communication. It is private, and cannot be measured without the honest participation of the individual.

In contrast to this, the Upper Right quadrant is the domain of the 'objective' or 'external' individual, and indicates the individual's physical and neurological wellbeing, health and development. This is what the thought looks like from the exterior of the individual who is thinking it. It might include the specific measurement of a pattern of brainwave activity, a localised neural firing in certain parts of the cerebral cortex, and perhaps a subtle flaring of the nostrils and/or movement of the eyes as the person visualises the pasta. This is the experience of the observer watching the individual who is having the thought with whatever apparatus they are using to observe, be it their five senses or multi-million-dollar machine extensions of their five senses. This is the physical correlate of the interior experience of having the thought.

Importantly, in the Upper Left quadrant, the intentional stance does not know the neural patterning or brainwave activity. It knows its own experience directly, without knowledge of the mechanical/organic transformations that correspond to the thought. On the other hand, in the Upper Right quadrant, the behavioural stance has no information about the nature of the actual, human experience involved with the set of neural firings and brainwave activity it is observing. No matter how detailed and patterned the quantitative descriptions of the exterior activity of the individual claiming to think about a certain phenomenon or idea, the behavioural stance can never know what it is like to experience the thought except by trying it on in one's own consciousness (Upper Left quadrant).

This is a crucial point, and needs emphasis. Although we can gain ever-finer appreciation of the interlinking patterns between the interior, intentional or conscious experiences of an individual and the exterior, behavioural and physiological correlates of those experiences, we can never reduce one to the other. They are fundamentally different and distinct orders of experience. For example, it doesn't matter how thoroughly we track the neural patterns in the brain or the chemical reactions on the tongue associated with the eating or remembering of a certain food; we can never actually experience the taste of that food by studying the exterior elements. With this under-standing, we can realise that reductive materialism and reductive idealism are fundamentally flawed as methods for understanding and explaining experience. This is why Wilber's model seeks to emphasise an understanding of our realities in terms of various aspects and how they interrelate, arguing that to concentrate on one to the exclusion of another gives a distorted and unhelpful version of the world and our place within it.

The Upper Left and Upper Right quadrants are therefore separate and distinct means of apprehending an experience. They are two openings through which we experience reality, and both must be considered if we are to have what Wilber calls 'integral' knowledge on any subject.

Notice also that for every Upper Left quadrant experience, there will be an Upper Right quadrant correlate, though not necessarily vice versa (the Upper Right quadrant shifts may not register on our five senses, or may be so subtle as to elude our awareness of them). As our measuring devices for the physical/neural activity of the human body have become more complex and sensitive to more subtle electrical and biochemical changes, we have registered systematic patterns of response associated with both thoughts and emotions. For example, there are distinct brainwave shifts (Upper Right) observed in subjects in deep hypnosis or meditation that correspond to the depth of trance or meditative awareness they report (Upper Left). Such examples are numerous and the more sensitive and precise our instrumentation becomes, the more subtle the Upper Left experiences we will be able to register and study. In the reverse, gross stimulation of brain neurons is sometimes associated with memories, thoughts and emotional content, while changing our biochemistry though the use of certain drugs or alcohol has a marked and well-documented effect on the human organism's interior experience.

The Lower Quadrants – The Collective Internal and External

So the two upper quadrants represent the interior and exterior manifestations of an individual. But individuals always exist and operate within collectives – we are unavoidably part of the systems, cultures and society into which we are born or within which we choose to exist. There is no inside without an outside, and no singular without a plural. Thus the lower two quadrants represent the plural – the collectives or communities of individuals. And, like individuals, these collectives or societies can be looked at from within and from without.

Therefore, whereas the upper quadrants are the seat of the individual's development, the 'I' or 'It', the lower quadrants consider the external aspects of our existence, the 'We' or 'Its'. The Lower Left ('We') marks the collective consciousness of which the individual is a part and which the individual has internalised; for example, our religious lives or the beliefs and values of the society, community or organisation of which we are a part.

The Lower Left quadrant therefore represents the shared world of meanings within groups and cultures, specifically our intersubjective and interpersonal meanings. At least in modern humans, much of our meaning is generated and conveyed through language. While Upper Left meanings and Lower Left meanings are certainly interdependent, certain personality functions are more interpersonal or rely more heavily on culture to supply their worldview or interpretations. Fields such as hermeneutics, semiotics, history, anthropology and religious studies are dedicated to further elucidating this intersubjective realm.

In contrast, the Lower Right ('Its') focuses on the external manifestations of that internal consciousness, specifically how the group organises itself and the relative level of sophistication of that organisation. Considering the world through the perspective of the Lower Right quadrant necessitates a focus on systems involving collections of entities: societies, economies, ecosystems etc. Like the Upper Right quadrant, observation and formalised, quantitative measurement are commonplace in approaches which seek to understand the Lower Right. Therefore, whilst the Lower Left focuses on meanings and other inner experiences that emerge from such collectives, the Lower Right describes their characteristics and mechanisms as viewed from without.

So the left quadrants are the internal, the right represent the external. The upper quadrants represent the individual, the lower quadrants the collective. However, what it is important to emphasise again at this point is the developmental and evolutionary ethos of Wilber's theory, which is central to the integral approach to facilitating the growth and development of our clients' wealth and the underlying principle of our management of our clients' family offices.

The AQAL Model as Developmental and Evolutionary, Not Static and Reactionary

Wilber's theory draws heavily on Spiral Dynamics,[4] which considers the interrelationship between the various aspects of our existence, and also how human functioning and growth is fundamentally developmental. However, the holistic and holarchic approach emphasised by Wilber is sophisticated and opens the possibility of considering the 'big picture' when it comes to family offices. At the same time, we share Frank Visser's belief that 'the Wilber debate ... should be critical, public, free, reasonable, informed, well-referenced, transparent, accessible and open to anyone who has studied Wilber'[5] and, as such, we have provided here a link to literature which is more critical of Wilber.

Integral Consulting and the AQAL Model

In terms of how these theories, or worldviews, inform our approach, we hold that in order to provide the best for our clients and to enable the achievement of the maximum potential for them, we must consider all aspects of the individual, as well as all aspects of the environment and cultures in which that individual exists, in order to understand our clients fully.

Through considering the management of our clients' family offices on All Quadrants, All Levels, our approach is systematic and deliberately integral, incorporating a range of considerations which enable us to fully match our clients' needs.

The ways in which the different aspects of the family office fall within the AQAL model are set out below, and, in keeping with Wilber's model, what is included within this framework is everything from previous models, plus additional factors which would not usually be considered systematically within the management of family offices. These aspects include the psychological health of the individual family members, the systemic health of the organisations around the individuals and how, in order to develop wealth, the organisations responsible must also develop in terms of their level of sophistication, with all quadrants developing and enforcing the development of the other quadrants.

Upper Left (Internal Individual)	Upper Right (External Individual)
Internal ambitions, intentions, hopes, fears, personal ethics and morals Level of consciousness Individual personal development and goal setting Ability to tolerate and process individual stress Philanthropy Psychological development	Health of the individual (physical and psychological) The physical body Experience of emotions, neurological connectivity, behaviours
Organisational culture Appropriate setting of goals for the organisation as a reflection of the ethics of the individuals within it Ability of the organisation to tolerate stress or adversity, learn from it and adapt	Systemic health of the organisation Structure and running of the organisation Wealth management and selection of the right options for growth Appropriate selection of experts and key personnel Ability of the organisation to adapt and grow
Lower Left (Internal Collection)	Lower Right (External Collection)

The Integral Approach to Wealth Management

Adopting an integral approach to wealth management enables us to consider the essential principles of successful wealth management in a way which takes into account the whole picture and allows the family office to take charge of its own future.

As Warren Buffett declared, in wealth management the mantra is, 'Rule No. 1: never lose money. Rule No. 2: never forget Rule No. 1.'[6] We hold to this as the underlying foundation of all approaches to successful wealth management, but our approach answers the question, 'Well, yes – but how do we make sure it works, for now and for the longer term?'

In considering the family office as a holarchic system with separate but interlinking dimensions, all of which will impact upon the overall efficacy of the structure which is put into place, the integral approach succeeds in aligning family and business interests with effective wealth-building goals and strategies whilst capitalising on the family's combined resources and skills within a meritocratic structure. What is created is a culture of accountability where simplicity is favoured when possible, but complexity is not avoided through fear or a lack of understanding, the importance of which is underlined by Stuart E. Lucas (2012) in his book, *Wealth: Grow It and Protect It*.

Through the focus on both the individual and the external structure in both the present and the future, there is also concentration on the development of current and future family leaders with strong wealth management skills to enable appropriate independence of the family office as a distinct entity, rather than, as is so often the case, an over-reliance on external consultants.

Understanding wealth management in terms of the AQAL map allows us to distinguish between beliefs and actions, between internal processes and external systems or structures, and to ensure that there is alignment between the two. Taking the view that any wealth management strategy is only as successful as its weakest parts, integral consulting attends to all dimensions of the process and integrates them, ensuring that longevity is guaranteed through building wealth management structures on solid foundations.

Summary: The Integral Approach

Integral consulting is able to assess, establish, organise and manage the clients' family offices in the manner which best meets their needs. We consider our clients' needs, wishes and goals, both personal and financial, within the developing and evolving context of their families, communities and society, and we conceive of our clients' family offices as inextricably linked to the individuals, but also shaped by the contexts and systems in which they operate. We understand that a family office is a reflection of both the internal and the external development of both the individuals of which it is made and the wider organisational structure.

Integral consulting's investment thesis is based on long-term financial stability, achieved through thinking in terms of the implications of investment in a 'holarchic' way, considering the appropriateness and value of investments for the individuals and organisations.

As explained earlier, our approach intends for long-term financial growth and stability but also for the growth and stability of our clients' family offices in terms of culture, organisation and levels of functioning, and we will therefore set out how Integral Investing achieves this added value through considering our clients and their future plans in a holistic and holarchic way.

Chapter 5 – A quick reference guide:

1. To understand the whole picture, we need to consider the whole picture, rather than looking at parts separately.

2. A family office is made up of all four elements in the All Quadrants, All Levels model (individuals and organisations considered both 'internally' and 'externally'). To understand them, and how they each connect to and either enhance or inhibit the others, is key to success.

3. A family office, like the family it represents and serves, should be a dynamic organisation which is always developing.

Notes and References: Chapter 5

[1] See, for example, Wilber, K. (2001) *A Theory of Everything: An Integral Vision for Business, Politics, Science and Spirituality*, Boston, MA: Shambhala Publications, and Wilber, K (2000) *Integral Psychology*, Boston, MA: Shambhala Publications.

[2] Author of *Beyond Individualism: Reconstituting the Liberal Self* (1989) Oxford: Oxford University Press.

[3] See, for example, Young, J.E. (2002) 'A Spectrum of Consciousness for CEOs: A Business Application of Wilber's Spectrum of Consciousness'. *International Journal of Organisational Analysis* 10(1), 30–54.

[4] See, for example, Beck, D. (2003) *Spiral Dynamics: Mastering Values, Leadership and Change*. Malden, MA: Blackwell Publishing.

[5] For a collection of critical articles and opinions on Wilber, see Visser (2014 and various), 'My Critical Essays on Ken Wilber'. http://www.integralworld.net/visser25.html.

[6] Loiacono, S. (2010) 'Rules That Warren Buffet Lives By'. Yahoo! Finance, February 23rd. http://finance.yahoo.com/news/pf_article_108903.html.

Family Businesses and Family Offices: Three Case Studies

Introduction

From Paris Hilton to Hans Kristian Rausing to the next-generation members of other high-profile wealthy families, such as those of Carlos Slim and Michael Bloomberg, who are seeking to find ways to continue the family's (and their own individual) wealth and success, the transition of the family wealth between generations is often problematic.

As we described in earlier chapters, the story of family businesses and wealth is a story of the challenges facing different generations, with their different understandings of and attitudes towards money, work and wealth, and their different relationships to the family office despite, crucially, being linked by their membership of the family in question. This chapter sets out, in practical terms, some of the issues facing multi-generational family businesses and family offices, explaining why it is essential for family businesses, including family offices, to consider a range of potentially conflicting influences on the success of their operations. These include the individual family members and their relationships to each other and to the family's wealth, as well as the external systems which are in place to ensure both stability and growth over multiple generations.

In this chapter, we will use the 'four phases' of the family business which we described in Chapter 1 to demonstrate the difficulties and challenges facing families as they attempt to move wealth and sustain the success of the offices from one generation to another. Many of the difficulties are related to the different social, cultural and psychological realities of the different generations and their relationship with 'wealth' which we discussed in Chapter 4.

This approach to consulting is influenced by the philosophies of Ken Wilber which we described in Chapter 5. For those readers who chose to jump from Chapter 4 to this one, the case studies set out below should be fully understandable without reference to Chapter 5. However, for those readers who did choose to look at Chapter 5, these case studies can be considered from the perspective of how we need to consider all four 'quadrants' and all 'levels' of functioning for both the individuals and the organisational structures which exist.

To explain this integral approach, we have provided case studies which are representative of many of the most frequent issues we see as standing in the way of the long-term success of family offices.*

Case Study 1: Developing from a PFO to an SFO

Background

Richard was a successful entrepreneur whose businesses came into their own when Richard was in his forties. Richard had married in his mid-thirties and at the age of sixty-two, when he unexpectedly passed away, his three children ranged in age from twenty-five to nineteen years old. The eldest of these was James.

James personally inherited approximately $40 million from Richard and was also made responsible for the management of his two sisters' inheritances, also equalling approximately $40 million each.

---

* Disclaimer: The examples included here as case studies are fictionalised composites based on a large number of different sources and are intended to enable the reader to understand some of the challenges facing our clients. Any resemblance to actual individuals is therefore entirely coincidental.

However, the inheritance was primarily comprised of real estate assets, trusts and business interests and so there was no real 'individual' inheritance but instead a shared inheritance between the three siblings of an equal part of $120 million. This inheritance had not been preceded by succession planning, in part due to Richard's age and sudden death, and the age of his eldest child at the time of his passing. James did not feel as if he had the tools or financial skills and abilities needed to manage the funds.

Up until the inheritance event, it may have seemed as if the structure of Richard's wealth was a single family office or SFO, but in reality the family's wealth had essentially functioned as a principal family office or PFO, serving Richard's needs and enabling him to directly meet the needs of his children.

At the time of inheritance, only James was (recently) married but it was highly likely that within the next decade all three siblings would be married and have children of their own. As such, the family office was in a situation where, within thirty years, the family would include not only a third generation, but also potentially a fourth.

There was already stress on the relationships between James and his sisters. James was trying to manage the fund on his own, struggling to establish relationships of trust with expert finance professionals. The PFO structure which had suited the family when Richard was alive and the three siblings were younger was no longer appropriate due to the increasingly independent and geographically diverse lives of the now-adult children. The sisters and, to an extent, their mother were frustrated at effectively having their financial needs met directly by James, and the system that had worked when Richard had been the head of the family was now in need of reorganisation.

James and his immediate family members, in particular his wife and younger sisters, needed to re-establish trust within their relationships. Whilst this was initially difficult, James managed to develop the ability to communicate his worries to them. In turn, they came to understand that they had misinterpreted any lack of communication as arrogance or an attempt to exclude them, rather than coming from James's deeply held sense of responsibility.

Once these relationships were improved, James was able to move to the second stage: a thorough assessment and diagnosis of the family's combined and individual goals, plans and hopes for the future. Establishing both shorter- and longer-term plans would enable James to develop the culture of the family office, which would likely include philanthropy, investment and the encouragement of business interests alongside long-term growth of the fund.

Crucially, this second stage needs to involve the detailed drafting of the family office's governance documents which set out the intentions, goals and principles of the family's financial management structures. In this case, this was a structure which, under Richard's leadership, was intended to work effectively as an SFO and would ensure that the family's wealth was able to provide directly for James, his mother whilst she was still living, his two sisters and their own children. Whilst long-term planning is key, the structure of the family office would at some point need to change again to adapt to the growing numbers of family members and their inevitably more distant relationships with each other.

What James also felt he needed was executive coaching to help him develop his ability as the chairman of the family office, in terms of both his general financial knowledge and his emotional skills. Coaching and training enabled him to drive forward the creation of an organisation which made appropriate use of experts and had sound governance in place – including due diligence and effective cost management and accounting procedures.

As a next step, the development of James's financial and management skills was taken to the next level to ensure that both he and the family office itself were taking steps which were appropriate to their relative level of development and did not overreach themselves. For example, whilst James initially decided that he wanted to invest in a large and established manufacturing business (and the opportunity presented itself within the first year of the family office's establishment), the level of investment in terms of personnel, time, expertise and money was not the right move for the family office at that juncture. To not invest at that time, despite his initial excitement and desire to do so, was a demonstration of the development of James's ability to make an accurate assessment of the family office's and his own personal capacity.

The final aspect of the development of the PFO into an SFO for James's family office involved philanthropy, in many ways something which may not seem to contribute to financial growth and an area where many, well-intentioned, activities do not have the impact which was intended. However, both morally and ethically it was important to James and his family to engage in philanthropic activities and the growth of the family's fund in the previous year now enabled this.

An area which can often be relevant is 'impact philanthropy', specifically considering areas which not only would be of interest to the family, but where the level of funds and time available would make a real difference, as intended. This will involve planning and the same balancing between the four different aspects of the family office as with the growth of the main fund itself.

James's family office is now in its third year and is continuing to flourish, both as a business and as a philanthropic organisation. The growth of the fund by approximately 10% per annum over the period is, in many ways, the tip of the iceberg. Under the surface of this are healthier family relationships and more effective and confident individuals whose abilities and skills, both financial and interpersonal, have increased. As a result of these and other internal factors, a family office structure has been developed which has strong governance and is capable of achieving long-term stability and growth.

Case Study 2: David and the Third-Generation Problem: Moving from an SFO to an MFO

Aged fifty, David had inherited control of family businesses established by his father, as well as a standing fund now worth approximately $140m. David had successfully established an SFO which had, for two decades, met the needs of himself, his younger sister (whom with David we shall call the 'second generation'), their respective spouses, and the 'third generation': his sister's family of two children and David's own family of four children, from two different marriages.

All of the third generation were now aged between thirty and fifty years of age with their own children (the 'fourth generation'). David was now in his early seventies and had recently become a great-grandfather, a happy development but one which drew his attention to the fact that what had been a relatively small family unit, which could be adequately served by the family office structure he had established two decades earlier, was now growing and beginning to include a fifth generation.

The combined family wealth was a healthy $180m, but David was aware that whilst he and his sister had equal shares of that, making their own personal wealth approximately $90m each, his four children would inherit only $22.5m each, and the fourth generation on David's side possibly only $5m individually, if the current structure persisted.

In addition to the issue of the gradually diminishing personal inheritances of each generation, David was also concerned with the question of management as he reached retirement. His daughter had expressed a desire for involvement but had no training in finance and he was concerned she lacked the necessary skills and personality to thrive in business. One of his sons-in-law (John) had also voiced a wish to become more central to the management of the family wealth, but whilst his personal skill set suited the needs of the family office,

John's relationship with David's daughter was not without issues and David was concerned for the stability of the family office should the relationship between his daughter and John deteriorate in the future.

The first need here is to understand the family's expectations and their belief and value systems, both as individuals and as a group, and any proposed plan of action must be in keeping with these.

David's focus was on the establishment of an early-stage multiple family office (MFO) but, initially, still under the umbrella of an SFO to avoid a dilution of the overall asset value and the income stream. The concept of 'better together' was one which David favoured both in terms of the efficiency of the organisational structure, and in terms of the ethos which fitted the family system he wished to enhance. The transition to an MFO was intended to take up to five years but would ensure that the family's wealth was not over-centralised, avoiding potential problems with competing demands on the funds from the various family members and their own claims on the inheritance.

David realised that with his niece, his nephew and his own four children, the structure would effectively need to be six 'devolved' single family offices with different individual values but without an outright division of assets.

David developed the governance documents to establish these structures, clarifying the intentions, goals and systems to be put in place to realise this. The medium-term goal was to enable the development of these individual units into a fully realised MFO, able to provide individually for the different families, but utilising the combined asset value for the benefit of all.

Case Study 3: MFO to Asset Management or MFO to SFO?

Nicholas was a 'third-generation' member of a wealthy family. He had grown up entirely within this environment and had no memories of a time when the family had not been so fortunate. This was in contrast to his father, Christopher, whose own experience of wealth had begun in his early teens when Nicholas's grandfather had managed to develop his businesses to the point where their lives changed substantially. Christopher had seen his father, Nicholas's grandfather, work incredibly hard throughout his life and, whilst Christopher was not as dynamic and intensely entrepreneurial as his father, he had a strong work ethic and a relatively grounded approach to the family's wealth. He had attended private schools for secondary education, but his primary education had been at the local state school and Christopher's father had encouraged him, from the age of fourteen, to take paid work during the holidays and on the weekends where possible.

This was in contrast to Nicholas, whose experience had been very different and is perhaps best described as set out by Elaine Rockefeller in her memoir.[1] Nicholas had personally inherited over $2m at twenty-one but spent almost all of it in three years and by his thirties, Nicholas was, aside from his potential future inheritance and income from his interest in the family office, almost broke.

Nicholas's grandparents and parents had, through hard work and significant ability, achieved a great deal but, as perhaps an inevitable consequence, Nicholas's own personal development, confidence and sense of his own ability had not grown at the same pace as the family's financial strength. Nicholas felt inadequate compared to his parents and his poor behaviour was rooted in a lack of internal development, poor self-esteem, a lack of accurate self-awareness and emotional intelligence, and his family's difficulties in understanding him.

Again, in this case, family dynamics and the difficulties for securing long-term family wealth are key issues. Although his parents had been hugely successful, without Nicholas developing the ability to sustain and continue the stability and growth of the family's businesses, the wealth of this family could be lost within the next generation and the structure of the family office would need either to develop into an asset management structure, likely to be run by a CEO who was not a member of the family, or to be split between individual families with either total or partial separation from the MFO.

The SFO option was, for Nicholas, not seen as practicable and would effect an even more extreme dilution of the family's overall assets and wealth than an asset management structure. Nicholas's father therefore faced a further dilemma. He believed that Nicholas had potential and wished, as far as possible, to keep ownership and control of the family's businesses within the family itself, but the question was whether to begin a process of transition from an MFO to professionalised asset management or not.

The approach taken focused on developing Nicholas personally, helping him to 'catch up' in terms of firstly his emotional intelligence and then his self-esteem and awareness of his own capacity. The relationship with his family, who were involved in the process and (as is essential) supportive throughout, improved alongside Nicholas's growth and the trust and communication within the family became significantly more healthy.

As part of the succession planning, Nicholas's father, after a period of time, invested in a start-up business in which Nicholas was interested. This allowed Nicholas to further develop his practical skills in business, financial and organisational management, whilst at the same time enabling a huge increase in self-confidence and further development of his relationship with his entrepreneurial father, who saw his son's potential as a successful businessman in his own right and a safe pair of hands in which he could ultimately trust the family wealth.

What is demonstrated by this is that succession planning is not an event but a process which may take several years and involves not only work on the robustness of the business's structures, but an investment in the individuals who are to take the helm.

Summary

In Nicholas's case, as with all the case studies presented here, whether the financial and business issues or the family dynamics were the reason for first noticing that things were becoming more difficult, what is clear is that the two sides of 'family' and 'office' cannot be considered as entirely separate from each other. The internal development of the individuals within the family and the subsequent external signs of this, including their behaviour and their relationships with others, have a direct impact upon the likely success of any family office. At the same time, there are the 'hard' facts of business which are often structural and organisational. Just as it cannot be assumed that if the family office is running successfully, all the family relationships will be healthy(!), it cannot be assumed that healthy individuals and good family dynamics will inexorably lead to successful business endeavours.

The different aspects are both separate and linked, and what our approach shows is that you cannot solely focus on one aspect and ignore the others. As traditional approaches to family office or family business management have shown, focusing on one aspect will have only limited success. Alex Polizzi (herself a very successful 'third-generation' individual) highlighted in her recent documentary series *The Fixer* that with family businesses you must look at both the family and the business and, unless you consider both, you will fail.

Family offices, by their very nature, are potentially vulnerable on all sides. Firstly, they are highly dependent on a relatively small number of individuals for success and the need for those individuals to be 'up to the job' is therefore key. This is in terms of their personal internal development but also how that internal development and capacity manifests in, for example, their behaviour, emotional and cognitive processing and their overall level of health. Family offices are also more vulnerable than almost any other endeavour to tensions within the relationships of those within the organisation, which can derail the businesses and prevent any possibility of either short- or long-term success. The family office is also vulnerable, as is any business, to external factors, global trends and weaknesses in structure or organisational functioning.

The approach outlined here treats all of these factors as of equal significance. Our approach understands that a family office is a four-legged table and recognises the need for integral consulting which addresses all four aspects – internal and external, individual and collective – as crucial factors in the potential success and long-term stability and growth of our clients' family offices.

Chapter 6 – A quick reference guide:

1. Try to analyse your family office in terms of the 'stage' it is at, and whether you think that stage is the most appropriate.

2. Individual skills development for the members of each generation is key – we need to understand their abilities, areas of difficulty and, crucially, what they need. So go through the key personnel, both current and future, and try to list their abilities and challenges. Then think how you could develop these with them.

3. The skills needed by a first-generation individual managing a PFO are not the same as those needed by a second-generation individual managing an SFO or MFO etc. The skills and structure of the family office need to be aligned to be most successful. Do yours match up appropriately?

Notes and References: Chapter 6

[1] Rockefeller, E. (2013) *Being a Rockefeller, Becoming Myself: A Memoir.* New York, NY: Blue Rider Press.

CHAPTER 7

The Solution –
The First Generation

The purpose of the next three chapters is to understand how we can have the most effective interventions to achieve the most successful family offices over multiple generations.

These chapters set out the natural states, without intervention, of the first, second and third (and fourth etc.) generations and look at how they differ from each other. The purpose is to consider the solution: how members of each generation can look at their own beliefs, expectations and experiences and identify both the strengths and weaknesses of their own natural states, with a view to both relating to the other generations and becoming the best they can be as individuals and as a family.

The intention is to look at the differences between the generations: to consider how the first generation can bring up the second generation effectively, preparing them for the challenges which they will face and helping them overcome the natural challenges which arise from the production of great wealth, then to look at how the second generation (often with the help of the first) can bring up the third generation in a way that will ensure they are successful and that they 'thrive'. These chapters are about having a conscious intention and way to overcome these challenges.

Importantly, the intention of these chapters is also to help the generations relate to each other better through an understanding of the key influences, neurology, psychology, and the beliefs and values of the other generations. However, these chapters have been written to stand alone if you're only looking for information on one generation, which means that there may be some slight repetition.

Briefly, what we describe is the natural state, without intervention, of the first generation, which is a state of 'relative poverty'. The first generation will usually be thinking about day-to-day expenditure and therefore caring about and recognising the value of money. It may be that they come from 'relative' rather than actual poverty, but by 'first generation' what we mean is the first generation whose wealth creation exceeds that of their parents or grandparents to the point where their situation changes significantly from that of their predecessors.

The second generation will have some of this experience and an awareness of how well their parents have done, but they have no actual need to consider daily expenditure or spending on everyday (or sometimes not-so-everyday!) items. Therefore these individuals have a mixed experience and their psychological processes, their sense of reward and motivation, their beliefs and behaviours are a reflection of this. In many ways, the second generation have one foot in each camp. However, the third generation will not naturally have this experience relating to the value of money, or of issues relating to daily expenditure.

The third generation will not have seen their grandparents before the wealth was created. Although they may have grown up in a house with a parent who shares some of the first generation's values around money, they will have been almost entirely 'abstract' values rather than 'real' daily considerations and there are no consequences or 'resistances' which assist the third-generation brain to wire itself in the same way as their grandparents'.[1] Therefore the third generation will need to be consciously and deliberately taught the value of money. The third generation, without being taught this consciously, will be unable to connect with concerns of their parents or grandparents surrounding the ethics and value of work and its relationship to money. This is not, as we've said before, because of any failing or flaw

– just that their life experiences are different and, therefore, so are they!

Personality and the First-Generation Wealth Creators

As discussed in the case of Robert, in Chapter 2, the first-generation wealth creators of any family are often (although not always) ambitious, highly intelligent and in possession of a dominant personality. This may be based on a variety of motivational factors, but what marks this generation out is that they are exceptionally driven. These are people who want to achieve something themselves and, regardless of where they come from (whether relative affluence or either extreme or relative poverty), they will be those who outstrip the generation which preceded them. The definition of the 'first generation' as wealth and business creators is that they have been able to create a level of wealth which far exceeds the level of everyday need – they are ultra-wealthy in that they no longer have to consider the cost of everyday living.

The first generation need to have an exceptional level of drive as they make many millions using a combination of hard work, intuition and a single-mindedness which may often mean that they can be perceived as ruthless. Being cautious, sensitive and hesitant are not usual characteristics of a first-generation wealth creator as their motivation would be elsewhere and their actions and drive centred on other things. In Myers-Briggs tests, the first-generation wealth creators often are characterised as INTJ ('Mastermind'), ENTJ ('Commander'), INTP ('Architect') or ENTP ('Inventor') personality types, and, although these are a generalisation and there are many variations within this, these types perhaps provide a helpful way to understand the motivations and driving forces of first-generation individuals and, of course, the way they are perceived by others.

At the same time, the characteristics which make these individuals successful can mean they are sometimes perceived as domineering, unforgiving and relentless. Sometimes, just being in the presence of such a person and having an awareness of what they have achieved can lead other people to feel 'less than'. First-generation wealth creators often have the ability to identify another's weaknesses or inadequacies, as part of the range of skills which have enabled them to succeed. But this can be difficult around the boardroom table, and even more difficult around the family dinner table (the effect of which on second-generation wealth 'preservers' is something which we discuss in Chapter 8).

Whilst perhaps overly simplistic, what this 'personality sketch' shows is that first-generation wealth creators have the characteristics necessary for success, but that these may bring with them a host of unintended consequences for family, for their business and organisational structures, and for the passing of their wealth and the control of the businesses to the second and subsequent generations.

Maslow's Hierarchy of Needs

Considering the personality of the typical first-generation wealth creator and using Maslow's hierarchy of needs as a starting point (see Chapter 3), a child who is born into a family where there is a need to consider whether or not there is enough money to meet daily expenditures will experience a deficit in the area of Maslow's hierarchy which relates to security. That deficit will be remembered by the individual and will be formative, psychologically and, crucially, neurologically (which we consider more below).[2] The formative nature of these experiences essentially comes from the fact that there is a level of insecurity (either current or historic) which is established in respect of our needs. Using Maslow's argument, when this insecurity is ingrained, the perceived 'lack' on which that insecurity is based will never entirely disappear, despite a change in circumstances. It is a sense of 'lack' that originates internally rather than externally and is therefore based not on external circumstances but on an internal sense of need. This is what J.K. Rowling and Oprah were expressing in their discussion on whether they ever 'feel rich'.

What may also suffer, in the pursuit of financial and business success, are personal relationships – it is often simply not possible to be managing a growing and successful set of enterprises whilst also being fully engaged in family life or developing friendships. Thus, whilst the first-generation wealth creators may appear to have achieved all levels of Maslow's hierarchy, in actual fact there are potentially insecurities which are present in what Maslow sees as the different levels of need (again, see Chapter 3 for a full description of Maslow's theory of the hierarchy of our needs).

Take, for example, Peter, the client discussed in Chapter 4 who remembers being deprived as a child, surviving on cereal with water and bread with no butter, and for whom that remembered deprivation is motivational. Although an extreme example, part of his success and his drive is founded on ensuring that, as an adult, he will not be without necessities again – but in this, he arguably overcompensates, to the point where he could buy a bakery, not just a loaf of bread. The point is that the remembered deprivation is not 'rational', and cannot be quantified. When we have been without our basic needs, nothing will be enough to remove the insecurity completely and we will continue to strive to meet that need, even when rationally we know that the 'lack' is no more.

Another part of Peter's success comes through the lack of a sense of belonging. It is the detachment he feels from his peers and his family which enables him to be more 'ruthless' than others. Having had a difficult relationship with his violent stepfather, Peter states that unlike the rest of his family, who still live within a two-block radius of each other, he moved away and does not want to go back. What, you may ask, makes Peter's siblings different from him? Surely, if the circumstances of his upbringing inspired him, they would inspire his siblings? But, of course, it does not work like this and it is a combination of his individual life experiences (alongside the shared ones), perhaps other factors such as birth order (Peter is the oldest boy, but not the eldest child) and, crucially, natural ability and talent that makes Peter different from his siblings.

It is not that Peter does not have friends and does not love his family; he does. Instead, it is that meeting the perceived need on levels 1 and 2 of Maslow's hierarchy of needs (physiological and safety needs) will always take precedence over belonging (albeit through an unconscious rather than conscious set of choices). And therefore, whilst Peter would appear to have moved into meeting the levels of need relating to fulfilment or 'self-actualisation', he would argue, much like J.K. Rowling or Oprah, that he does not 'feel' rich and is aware how close the margin often is between success and failure.

He does not relax into his success but instead he feels it is always precarious, and this is one reason why it is likely that Peter, like Robert, will continue working well past normal retirement age. Because the idea of an income which is 'passive' (from investments or interest on capital) rather than 'active' (i.e. one over which he can exert a direct influence and put in extra time and effort where needed) provokes that intrinsic insecurity which may never fully leave him.

Another reason why Peter may struggle to 'give up' work, like Robert, is that his 'esteem needs' (level 4 of Maslow's hierarchy of needs) are met by his sense of self as a successful business person and entrepreneur. It is this sense of self on which Peter's self-esteem is built. He is no longer the child at whom the other kids laughed because his clothes were bought from charity shops and discount retailers, or the child who was unable to help as his mother was ill-treated by her partners; he is someone who has achieved success in life, and that success (and others' perception of it) makes him safe, and of value. His appearance and the outward markers of that success are therefore also important to him (cars, suits, the attractiveness of his partner, etc.). Essentially, his self-esteem is based on a sense of this 'successful' person, whilst Peter outside this role is perhaps not worth as much. It is a conditional valuing of self which makes retirement and handing over control of the family's wealth and businesses particularly problematic.

To discuss this in terms of Maslow is not to say that Maslow has all the answers or that this approach is the 'right' one. Maslow's approach is humanistic and considers only our lived experiences as influential (rather than our innate biological or neurological structures). However, thinking of things in these terms can be helpful in enabling us to understand what may be going on underneath the surface and why we find ourselves pulled towards certain activities, engaged by some things and not others, based on our formative experiences.

Neurological Development

The external indicators such as those described above are simply that: the external indicators. Our beliefs, values and behaviours are a consequence of our neurological structures which have developed in response to particular circumstances. Maslow's approach considers our lived experiences but does not connect these directly to the influence on our neurological development.[3] Whilst our brains remain somewhat plastic until our middle age, the fact is that it is during our younger years when they are most able to respond to changing external circumstances and adapt accordingly. They are not called 'formative' years for nothing!

As such, our experiences and influences in our childhood, adolescence and young adulthood are crucial in forming our neurological structures which, in turn, dictate how we prioritise, motivate ourselves and relate to other people (and the wider world around us). Therefore what we describe as the natural characteristics of the first, second and third generations are related to neurological structures and how they have developed.

In members of the first generation, reward mechanisms and anxiety triggers will respond differently to thoughts of work and money from those of the third generation. The first generation's reward structures will be highly motivated towards the creation of wealth and thoughts of being without, or of returning to a less affluent financial state, will create a state of relative physical and emotional anxiety (which is a motivator to resolve or take action).

Our neurological structures inform our priorities, guide what drives us and govern what engages our interest. The first generation's choices are governed by their neurological response to the concept of money and its uses, the idea of work, and how those are prioritised over such things as physical fitness, relationships with friends or, on a more specific level, the thought of attending parents' evenings or school plays. Of course, it is possible to 'choose' differently (to attend a parents' evening rather than a business meeting), but the sense of reward and the reduction in anxiety, the feeling of engagement and the 'importance' associated with the two events will be directed by our neurological structures.

The structures have been formed as a response to previous events and experiences, particularly during childhood, adolescence and young adulthood. These events and experiences will have caused neuro-chemical levels to change, and it is these changes and fluctuations in our neurochemistry which then dictate the way our brain 'wires itself'. Therefore, although we are free to 'choose', our neurological structures will push us towards making some choices rather than others.

The point of looking at this generational question from a neurological point of view is to emphasise that none of the characteristics or states of the first, second and third generations are 'better' or 'worse' than the others. It is to acknowledge that they are a consequence of upbringing, events and experiences which have not just affected behaviour and belief systems on a superficial level, but also will have created neurological structures or 'wiring' which then dictate how the different generations approach situations and what they are motivated by.

If we understand that neurologically the reward pathways of the first and third generation will, in their natural state – without intervention – have very little in common due to the very different formative experiences of the two generations, it is no wonder that there is often a lack of common understanding and a lack of a sense of how to be of help.

Psychology and Behaviour

In this book, we separately discuss the neurological and psychological, but, of course, the two are inextricably linked. We want to highlight that our psychology (our sense of reward, what makes us happy, what causes anxiety, what engages and interests us) has its roots in neurological structures which are developed in our childhoods.

Therefore, the intervention which takes place to assist the various generations must take into account that a psychological approach (or any psychological aspects of intervention) will, if successful, have an effect on our neurological structures, and a change in psychology will be as a result of (and contribute towards) 'rewiring' of those structures.

That said, the psychological state of the first generation and their behaviour will be different from those of the second and third generation – as a consequence of what we have set out above. It is a first-generation characteristic that happiness (either overt or a quieter sense of what might be closer to 'satisfaction') is obtained through achievement. A sense of achievement is key for first-generation wealth creators and, of course, the neurological structures of the brain are wired to experience pleasure from (and therefore to be motivated towards) achievement. First-generation individuals are often highly goal-orientated – business, sport, music or really any other task is always approached with commitment and determination. This is, at least in part, because the fear of failure (or, more accurately, the fear and grounded awareness of the consequences of failure) is stronger in first-generation individuals than in those of subsequent generations.

A first-generation individual usually will want to be the best at most things, not because they like to make the rest of us aware of our flaws(!) but simply because if an achievement is possible, they will work towards it fiercely. What would be the point, to a first-generation individual, of attempting anything unless they were going to give it 100%? To quote George Mallory when asked why he climbed Everest, despite the challenges and dangers, 'Because it was there.'

At the same time, it may be difficult for a first-generation individual to understand that their sons and daughters may not want to climb Everest just because it is there waiting to be climbed. They may perceive that apparent lack of ambition or motivation to succeed as laziness, weakness, or lacking drive. But, as we shall consider when looking more at second-generation individuals, it is not unusual for children of high-achieving parents to be significantly less motivated by the idea of 'achievement', particularly in relation to money (and their children, the third generation, even less so).

In considering the psychology and behaviour of first-generation individuals as geared around their own reward pathways, we can begin to understand why it is often difficult for first- and second-generation individuals to see eye-to-eye. The impact on the family businesses and wealth management, as well as the family's long-term relationship quality, is immeasurable.

Social Structures and Organisational Structures

The social and organisational structures that are put in place by the first-generation wealth creators will likely be primarily patriarchal and centred around one person, rather than collaborative or truly democratic. This is the type of structure which tends to work well when business operations are first established. The centralisation of control around one person is, of course, appropriate for small and medium-sized businesses for a variety of practical reasons including, crucially, directing the success of the enterprise and keeping costs at a minimum.

The centralisation of control in the hands of one person is typical of a business set up by a first-generation wealth creator for all the reasons discussed above. However, what are often non-financial significant factors driving the creation of the business around one central figure are the esteem which comes from being a successful person, the neurological structures which detect reward, and the personality type of the individual.

Importantly, as discussed, the neurological structures, personality and psychology of the individual do not just emerge by accident but instead develop over time as a response to events, experiences and learnings. Crucially, as well as often coming from a more traditional background than the one in which they bring up their children (as many of us living in the West find), the fact that the first-generation individual's businesses first flourish (and the reward mechanisms are put in place) through them being in overall control of a centralised model of business means that altering this to include, for example, other family members on an equal footing goes against their natural sense of what 'works', which is linked to their reward systems.

This instinctive reluctance to share control may ensure business continuity in the short term; however, it is, of course, problematic in the medium to long term. What is not put in place is a succession plan whereby the second generation are included in the business processes and prepared, over the long term, to enjoy the sense of achievement, reward and satisfaction which comes from having a sense of ownership and of making a contribution to a family business.

Although the first generation do not intend to create a second generation who do not share their values and sense of reward, this is inadvertently what they do. The purpose of intervention with first-generation individuals, therefore, is to help them realise that they accidentally create a second generation who do not have the same sense of achievement and reward as they do.

Our intervention with first-generation wealth creators who wish to ensure the continuing success of their businesses therefore starts from the point of acknowledging that the wealth is already there and success already achieved, so the factors which influenced them are not going to be the same for their children. Instead, the purpose is for the first generation to help prepare their children for that fact – 'We already have the wealth and we have a successful family business, so what do you want to achieve and how can I help that happen?'

Helping the second generation to develop their own motivators, drives and ambitions from as early an age as possible is key. For first-generation individuals, it may be difficult to acknowledge that their children will inevitably see things differently. However, without this being established up front, a change in the natural inclinations will be impossible. And it is crucial that the motivators, drives and ambitions are the children's own, not those of their parents. Inherited ambition is not the same as primary ambition and will always be a diluted version of the original. Hence why the second generation are often seen as wealth preservers rather than entrepreneurs or creative forces in their own right – if they take over the family business (eventually), it is with the idea that their purpose is to continue their parent's legacy and maintain the successes of the previous generation, but this is an impossible task for all the reasons we have set out and is an essentially conservative motivation (which is antithetical to any idea of entrepreneurship or a creative drive).

Instead, if the first generation wish to ensure that their children (and eventually their grandchildren) are able to thrive and that the businesses and wealth they have worked so hard to grow do more than survive, the first step is to acknowledge that the very success they have achieved has immediately changed things for the generations which are to follow. These changes will be social, cultural, environmental, psychological and neurological and will influence every aspect of how the following generations will approach almost all situations, from the most simple to the most complex of tasks or interactions.

Moving from 'wealth creators' to 'creators of a successful second generation' will require work on the part of the first generation to look at how they can encourage motivation and a sense of reward (the latter being crucial if the former is to be achieved). One way in which this can be done is to look at their plans for the inheritance of wealth and the continuation of the business and consider, for example, whether, as Sting, Michael Bloomberg and Warren Buffett have done, they want to be clear that the second generation will not inherit anything at all.

But whatever the position taken on inheritance, it is important that this is communicated to the next generation clearly and consistently. If the intention is to pass on the wealth and running of the businesses to the next generation, then the first-generation individual must learn to go against their natural instinct and delegate effectively, share ownership and encourage creativity and ambition in their children.

Chapter 7 – A quick reference guide:

1. 'First-generation' individuals are creative and innovative. Their sense of reward is wired towards achieving more than those who have gone before them and creating something significant.

2. Alongside this, 'first-generation' personality types are usually leaders or 'commanders' and they do not require the approval of others to pursue their ambitions. Their 'frame of reference' is internal, rather than external.

3. The skills 'first-generation' individuals need to learn to help with the successful transition of wealth between generations include the ability to encourage others to feel 'successful' and to have ownership over the family's wealth. If their children do not feel ownership and control, they will not develop the skills to innovate or 'grow' the family's wealth – which may include taking it in a different direction as the economic climate changes.

4. If you are a first-generation individual, think about how you can encourage others to feel successful and have more ownership over the family office. How do you feel about retirement and allowing the next generation to truly take the reins?

5. For first-generation individuals nearing traditional retirement age (or well past it!), consider drawing up a three-year plan for handing over control. Do you feel the businesses will be well managed without you? If not, why not and what needs to happen?

Notes and References: Chapter 7

[1] Stiles, J. (2008) *The Fundamentals of Brain Development: Integrating Nature and Nurture.* Cambridge, MA: Harvard University Press.
[2] Kendrick, D.T., et al. (2011) 'Renovating the Pyramid of Needs: Contemporary extensions built on ancient foundations'. *Perspectives in Psychological Science* 5(3), 292–314.
[3] Ibid.

CHAPTER 8

The Solution –
The Second Generation

So, the first generation are 'wired' towards creation of wealth and innovation. They are driven, ambitious and determined, with a natural reluctance to share control. For the second-generation child, you know this already because these are your parents, and you grew up with them . . .

For many reasons, which we will describe and discuss below, the natural second-generation 'state' is that of conservation and preservation, rather than innovation. Second-generation individuals are not usually risk-takers and are not normally driven by the need to create something 'new'. Crucially, however, from our point of view, these skills of conservatorship are a natural complement to the skills of their parents and, if developed correctly, can be a real asset to the family's wealth and the smooth and successful transition to the generations beyond, rather than being seen as 'second generation, second best'.

What we don't want to try and do is just make the second generation 'more like the first', which is what many interventions try to do. As well as being essentially impossible due to their life experiences and their neurological and resulting psychological and emotional states (which is why these interventions rarely work), this isn't necessary or desirable – despite what you first-generation individuals may think! First-generation individuals did what they did because of their own skill sets, abilities, opportunities and environment. The second generation are different and therefore will do things differently, and our perspective is that this is a good thing, not a negative.

What we do want, however, is to enable the second generation to enhance their natural skills of conservatorship, loyalty, responsibility and preservation, alongside developing the awareness and skills to bring up a third generation which can value both the 'reality' and the opportunity of wealth and, crucially, then see themselves as important and active parts of a family office rather than passive recipients of a substantial benefits system. If the second generation can develop an understanding of their impact, both actual and potential, and how important they are to the family's wealth cycle (rather than seeing themselves only as temporary curators who will, at some point, be replaced by a successor), they will be able to transfer that understanding to their children.

Personality and the Second Generation

As with Josephine, Edward and Thomas in Chapter 2, the second generation can often struggle to establish themselves as individuals within the family system of business and wealth. They often see their role as 'continuing' what their parents have started and, in many cases, may resent this apparent predetermination of their life's plan. They didn't necessarily choose to be in business, and perhaps aren't even particularly interested naturally in business as a pursuit, but their sense of duty can mean they don't feel as if they have a voice, or a choice.

Whereas the first generation exploited their own natural abilities, along with opportunities which presented themselves, the second generation are coming into a structure which has already been created around them. 'Am I really interested in property, finance or technology and do I have the natural skills and aptitude to make a success of it?' These are not questions the second generation have the luxury of asking themselves if they are to fulfil their duty to their parents.

Whereas the first generation needed to have an exceptional level of drive, focused on a particular set of goals, the second generation who take up the reins of the family office require a different set of skills and abilities. They are facing a more complex and sophisticated set of problems than those which the first generation encountered, and their skills and approach to the problems need to reflect that. This is not in any way to minimise the achievements of the first generation but is intended to recognise that trying to balance wealth creation and preservation whilst honouring the achievements of one's parents – meaning that the second generation have to have an eye on both the past and the future – takes a specific set of abilities and should never be underestimated. This situation gets even more complicated when we get on to the third generation, but for second-generation individuals it is tricky enough!

Second-generation wealthy individuals are often more naturally cautious, sensitive and hesitant than their parents. Whilst, as we discussed in Chapter 7, the first-generation wealth creators often are characterised as ENTJ or 'Commander' personality types in Myers-Briggs tests, the second generation are often more likely to have developed skills around ISTJ or ISFJ types. In a different life, outside an ultra-wealthy family environment, these personality types are described as naturally drawn towards job roles such as the counsellor or the teacher, responsible and loyal, with a real sense of duty or 'doing what needs to be done'. They are the 'guardians' of the personality spectrum and do not naturally develop the skills of the 'front man' but instead are more likely to be best when supporting or helping to regulate others. As with the first-generation personality types, this is, of course, very generalised, but it fits with the natural tendency which is observed in second-generation individuals to feel that their role is to conserve and support, rather than to take risks or command others. This is partly an issue of what we describe as a sense of 'ownership'. If it is not 'mine', it is not mine to take risks with, and second-generation individuals often say that they do not feel they have real ownership over the family's wealth – they see themselves as tenants rather than landlords.

Financial decision-making requires quite a bit of objective and impersonal decision-making and not too much personal and subjective decision-making. A second-generation individual who tends to be more 'feeling' than 'thinking' will have experienced events and circumstances in a way which has emphasised this level of development. If you are the child of a determined 'thinking' type, it is often the case that the opposite skill set will develop – you can't outthink them objectively, but you can subjectively 'feel' something to be different. And you are perhaps not brought up with a sense that you can strike out on your own – your role is going to be to support and preserve someone else's vision because, in order to be the success that it has been, that vision has been all-consuming.

At the same time, the characteristics which make these second-generation individuals successful wealth preservers and conservators of their parents' legacies often mean they can be perceived as 'weaker' or less creative, without the ideas or strength of personality to push something through, or without the risk-taking nature sometimes needed to seize an opportunity. Being brought up by a high-achieving first-generation individual can lead many second-generation individuals to undervalue their own instincts or ideas, testing them against the 'known' successes of their parent or parents. And the result is usually a more conservative nature.

However, as we said earlier, our aim is not to change this beyond all recognition and create another first generation. That wouldn't work either. Instead, what we are advocating is recognising that there are real benefits to being naturally more of a 'preserver', and if combined with building of self-esteem and the valuing of these characteristics, the effect is an active and dynamic conservatorship with a real sense of ownership and direction, rather than a more passive, loyalty-driven guardianship of 'someone else's' wealth.

Maslow's Hierarchy of Needs

Considering the personality of the typical second-generation individual and using Maslow's hierarchy of needs as a starting point (see Chapter 3 and Chapter 7), a child who is brought up in a family where, at some point in their development, there ceases to be a need to consider whether or not there is enough money to meet daily expenditures will experience a fundamentally different world to their parents in the area of Maslow's hierarchy which relates to security. These experiences will be remembered by the individual and will be formative, psychologically and, crucially, neurologically (which we consider more below).

The formative nature of these experiences essentially comes from the fact that there is a level of basic security which is established in respect of the individual's needs. Their experience will obviously depend on the age they were at when their parents developed their significant wealth. However, they will likely have a personal memory of when life was different or will absorb their parents' remembered experiences of relative hardship, and, using Maslow's argument, this sense of 'valuing' the wealth and a certain level of insecurity in levels 1 or 2 of the hierarchy will remain, but in a more abstract way than for their parents. Due to the fact that the second generation are in possession of wealth as part of a family, but did not create it themselves and so have no experience of their own ability to create significant wealth (whilst, at the same time, they understand that 'to have is better than to be without'), the instinct becomes focused on preservation rather than the taking of risks which might undermine that security. A typical second-generation individual does not take risks with what often feels like 'someone else's money'.

Alongside this, they are the children of parents who often needed to prioritise business over family, perhaps meaning they were absent for significant periods of time. Second-generation individuals do not have the same direct sense of 'lack' in the first two levels of Maslow's hierarchy as their parents may have had, but instead their sense of lack may be more focused on the third level, of 'belonging', and therefore relationships are often of more importance to second-generation individuals (hence why they perhaps can seem to lack the ruthlessness of their first-generation predecessors). A second-generation individual grows up being very aware of others but often experiences their own needs as secondary at home, although this is perhaps not understood by others outside the home (for example, at school) where they appear to have everything they could want.

Peter, the first-generation individual discussed in chapters 4 and 7, admits that one of the things he finds most difficult is having a less senior member of his staff or someone who is younger than him disagree with or question his decisions. He states that he can be quite dismissive when this happens. He wants to try not to repeat this pattern with his children (of which he currently only has one, a son) as they get older, because he understands it would undermine their own confidence in their abilities and skills. But he knows it will be a difficult change to make. This because, as discussed in Chapter 7, for Peter as a first-generation individual, the perceived lack in levels 1 and 2 of Maslow's hierarchy of needs will always override the needs above. If he perceives a threat to his security, he will prioritise that over the relationship.

What Peter then helps to create is a second-generation individual who does not feel the same lack in levels 1 and 2 (despite understanding that lack), but whose focus is on level 3 of the hierarchy – aiming to preserve the relationship with the parent without undermining the security of levels 1 and 2. But this lack in the 'belonging' and relationship level will essentially undermine the development of the second-generation individual's self-esteem (level 4 of the hierarchy) to a greater or lesser extent, which will be based upon their ability to sustain the security in levels 1 to 3. The second generation self-esteem (level 4) is therefore founded on the success (or lack) in levels 1 to 3, none of which are taken for granted.

Neurological Development

As we described in Chapter 7, the external indicators such as personality described above are just that: external signs. Our beliefs, values and behaviours are a consequence of our neurological structures which have developed in response to particular circumstances. Maslow's approach considers our lived experiences but does not connect these directly to the influence on our neurological development. Our experiences and influences in our childhood, adolescence and young adulthood are crucial in forming our neurological structures which, in turn, create our 'personality structures' and our 'needs'. Therefore what we describe as the natural characteristics of the first, second and third generations are related to neurological structures and how they have developed, and our personalities and needs are a result of these.

For the second generation, reward mechanisms and anxiety triggers will respond differently to thoughts of work and money from those of the first or third generations. The first generation's reward structures will be highly motivated towards the creation of wealth, and thoughts of being without, or of returning to a less affluent financial state, will create a state of relative physical and emotional anxiety (which is a motivator to resolve or take action). For the second generation, reward structures will be more motivated towards preservation of wealth, taking fewer risks, consolidation and conservation – a valuing of the family's status quo after many years of change.

Our neurological structures inform our priorities, guide what drives us and govern what engages our interest. The second generation's choices are governed by their neurological response to the concept of money and its uses, the idea of work, and how those are prioritised (or not) over such things as relationships with others or self-esteem. Our neurological structures will direct the feeling of engagement and the 'importance' associated with the sometimes opposing or conflicting demands of taking firm decisions which could lead to an increase in wealth, versus the potential impact on our relationships.

These structures have been formed as a response to events and experiences in childhood, adolescence and young adulthood. As described in Chapter 7, these events and experiences cause neurochemical levels to change and it is these changes and fluctuations in our neurochemistry which then dictate the way our brain 'wires itself'. Therefore, although we are free to 'choose', our neurological structures will nudge us towards making some choices rather than others.

As Malcolm Gladwell's theory of the 'inverted U-shaped curve' of benefit states, due to the relatively small increase (if any) of perceived benefit once wealth is at a certain point, the reward for taking decisions which enhance wealth at the expense of other aspects of life is reduced. If there is less reward then there is less motivation, and the second generation's sense of reward associated with the creation of wealth is naturally less than the first generation's. This is not just the way the second generation 'feel' about it (although the emotional sense is of course there) but is 'hard-wired' into their neurological structures.

If we understand that neurologically the reward pathways of the second, first and third generations will, in their natural state – without intervention – have very little in common due to the very different formative experiences of the three generations, it is no wonder that there is often a lack of common understanding and a lack of a sense of how to be of help.

The 'reward' for the second generation is often structured around loyalty, duty, family relationships, belonging and doing what is expected of them, but there may be some frustration and resentment that this 'reward' is one which is limiting and can feel lacking in creativity, partly because this 'reward' is often dependent on others rather than being individually centred. A second-generation individual once described how he wanted to pursue his own ideas but knew he was 'better at shaping and preserving other people's' and this was a source of tension at times.

In terms of interventions, what is needed is to enhance a sense of achievement in the second generation's conservatorial skills and appreciate them as valuable. These skills are to be considered 'rewarding'. This enhances the sense of 'ownership' it is necessary to develop. The ability to take other people's ideas and to adapt oneself to an already existing structure should not be underestimated and it is not a 'secondary' skill. At the same time, what would be of help to second-generation individuals would be to look at enhancing confidence in their own, independent abilities – to develop a sense that they can not only preserve well, but they can also have their own ideas and implement them. These ideas are not likely to be the risk-taking, more dramatic ones of the first generation, but they will add value.

In other words, intervention for the second generation is to enhance the skills they already have, but encouraging a modification of their neurological 'wiring' to give a similar sense of reward around their individual creativity and innovative abilities.[1]

Psychology and Behaviour

As we stated in Chapter 7, interventions which take place to assist the various generations must take into account that a psychological approach (or any psychological aspects of intervention) will, if successful, have an effect on our neurological structures and a change in psychology will be as a result of (and contribute towards) 'rewiring' of those structures.

The psychological state of the second generation and their behaviour will be different from those of the first and third generations, as a consequence of what we have set out above. It is a second-generation characteristic that happiness (either overt or a quieter sense of what might be closer to 'satisfaction') is obtained through consolidation rather than achievement. A sense of preserving and consolidating is key for second-generation individuals and, of course, the neurological structures of the brain are wired to experience pleasure from (and therefore to be motivated towards) this quietening of the pace of change. Second-generation individuals are not usually highly goal-orientated, but instead are often 'process-focused'. This is, at least in part, because they do not see themselves as being able to better the 'outcomes' achieved by the first generation, and therefore their abilities and interests are best suited and expressed when 'task'-related.

A second-generation individual will often highly value the way things are, and will want to help secure that. At the same time, a first-generation individual may find this difficult to understand and may see it as a lack of drive. It is important to understand that this tendency is not a lack of drive, but often lack of a psychological need to take unnecessary risks. This is, of course, alongside (as we said earlier) a lack of a sense of 'ownership' over the family's wealth. But this is not to say that second-generation individuals do not value achievement; they do as much as any other human being. It is just that what a second-generation individual considers an achievement will probably differ from those of the first generation. Interventions to help second-generation individuals are therefore best when they enhance this sense of achievement and encourage the setting of goals which match their natural skills and abilities, rather than setting goals which contradict these. With a sense that they are bringing value to the family office, enhancing and improving the organisation and achieving success in these ways, second-generation individuals will develop a sense of ownership. This sense of ownership will then enable the individuals to build on the consolidation of the family's wealth and take strategic decisions in a sophisticated and developed way.

In considering the psychology and behaviour of second-generation individuals as geared around their own reward pathways, it helps us to understand why it is often difficult for first- and second-generation individuals to see eye-to-eye. If understanding of these differences, and the opportunities these differences present, can be gained, then the family office can go from strength to strength.

Social Structures and Organisational Structures

The social and organisational structures that are inherited by the second generation will be those originally put in place by their parents. As we discussed in Chapter 7, these will likely be primarily patriarchal and centred around one person, rather than collaborative or truly democratic, because this is the type of structure which tends to work well when business operations are first established. The centralisation of control around one person is, of course, appropriate for small and medium-sized businesses for a variety of practical reasons including, crucially, directing the success of the enterprise and keeping costs at a minimum.

However, as the family wealth cycle moves into the second generation and then into the third, a patriarchal, relatively 'pared-down' organisational structure for the family office is not likely to work as effectively. As one example of why, the number of families included within the family office is now likely to be at least two or three, if not more. In some senses, it is no longer a 'family office' but now a 'families office'. Questions of who will take over the running, who is best suited (the eldest boy just by default?) and how this works in practice are all issues which the second generation have to deal with on a practical level. And this is often where the family office structure starts to fall apart, with the effects being felt by the third generation and beyond.

It is therefore crucial to realise that the wealth creation established by the first generation has presented the second generation with a more complex, more operationally sophisticated and more structurally nuanced problem than the first generation had to deal with. And this is why we say that the second generation is facing a real challenge. The previous approach to management will no longer work (or at least it will not work for long), and a sense of ownership and the ability to make sophisticated strategic decisions are key.

What can often happen is that the rate of growth that the first generation achieve means that the foundations are not quite adequate by the time the second generation take over. But the second generation are well-equipped to solidify this progress with their natural conservationist tendencies – as long as those skills are directed towards 'true' consolidation rather than simply a preservation of the status quo.

The first-generation instinctive reluctance to share control, as discussed in Chapter 7, may ensure business continuity in the short term; however, it is of course problematic for the second generation. What is not put in place is a succession plan whereby the second generation are included in the business processes and prepared, over the long term, to enjoy the sense of achievement, reward and satisfaction which comes from having a sense of ownership and of making a contribution to a family business. But if they are given this, the basis of the family's wealth will only be stronger, if not significantly larger, when the second generation take the reins.

Although the first generation do not intend to create a second generation who do not share their values and sense of reward, this is inadvertently what they do. And likewise, what a second generation who lack a sense of ownership, agency and faith in their own skills and abilities will then create are a third generation who are even more distanced from the sources of the wealth they enjoy. A second-generation individual who lacks a sense of their own destiny, subordinating that (sometimes willingly, sometimes resentfully) to preserving the achievements of their parents, will struggle to help develop a third-generation individual who has ambitions, a sense of value and any sense of connectedness with the reason people get up in the morning, spend the day at work and potentially sacrifice or, at the very least, delay gratification in favour of achieving personal goals.

In part, perhaps, it is the personality type which does not 'command' and the lack in the area of belonging (if seen in terms of Maslow's hierarchy) which means that second-generation individuals struggle to be directive towards their children. Perhaps also, a vicarious need to escape from the predestined role as guardians of the family office discourages second-generation individuals from encouraging the development of ambition, the ability to make sacrifices and the ability to delay gratification in their children. These are just two of a range of possibilities and any second-generation individual will, with the right interventions, be able to say why they, personally, struggle to enforce boundaries with their children – but we know that these boundaries are essential for the third generation to develop a sense of connectedness with valuing the limits which life puts on us.

As we said earlier, the second generation inherit a more complex set of problems than the first generation experience and this is nowhere more true than in family life. For the second generation, there were still some limits that were placed on life choices, but for the third generation (particularly where there is even more likelihood of never needing to be directly involved in the management of the actual family office), life is often not limited in the way that the majority of the world experience it. We will discuss this more in Chapter 9, but for the second generation, it is crucial that the ability to set firm limits for the third generation, from as early in life as possible, is enhanced.

Our intervention with second-generation individuals who wish to ensure the continuing success of the family's wealth, both in this generation and the next, and the happiness and wellbeing of their own children, therefore starts from the point of acknowledging that the solutions which worked for their parents are no longer applicable. If a second-generation individual has the confidence to say, 'Yes, but that solution no longer applies,' to their high-achieving parent, then we have made a start.

The second generation's role is to stabilise and preserve the wealth, but not through stagnation. Instead, it is to preserve through enhancing rather than just embalming the business! With confidence, a sense of ownership and a real sense of agency, this can be achieved.

At the same time, though, the second generation's role is to prepare the third generation for an even more complicated set of problems. The second generation's children will grow up in an environment where their concept of money and wealth, their 'psychology of money', will be fundamentally altered from that of their parents. The third generation's answer to the question 'what is money?' may be unrecognisable from that of the first generation, and it is key that the second generation understand that and make active choices as to how this will be managed. Do we, for example, limit the third generation's access to money through an allowance system which is strictly set (and enforced) in relation to the allowances of their school friends? Do we insist that they get a job on a weekend day so that they can learn what it is like to earn for themselves and gain an understanding of the 'ordinary' value of money? These are options, although they may feel unworkable for many second-generation individuals. For us, though, it is perhaps less important what actual strategies are employed than that something is done. The worst situation is where we give third-generation individuals access to whatever their hearts desire, but then criticise them for failing to appreciate the value of things. The second generation's role here is key, and is a real challenge.

If the second generation wish to ensure that their children (and eventually their grandchildren) are able to thrive and that the wealth created by their own parents will last beyond the third generation, the first step, as we said in Chapter 7, is to acknowledge that the very success their parents achieved has immediately changed things for the generations which are to follow. These changes will be social, cultural, environmental, psychological and neurological and will influence every aspect of how the following generations approach almost all situations, from the most simple to the most complex of tasks or interactions.

The second generation may feel that they fully understand the life experiences of the third generation, but the fact is that they naturally do not. They have not had the same lack of practical limitations on choice that their own children do, they have not had the same boundless opportunities, and they did not have themselves as parents!

And this emphasises our approach, which is to understand the factors which create first, second and third (and beyond) generations and to adapt the solutions to suit the challenges and opportunities for each of them individually, rather than adopting a 'one size must suit all' tactic which is doomed to fail by the time the third generation come of age.

The success of this hinges on the second generation. They are crucial and have far more potential power to influence than they often realise, and it is our belief that if they understand this and can adapt to it, there is no reason for the three-generation wealth trap to be sprung.

Chapter 8 – A quick reference guide:

1. 'Second-generation' skills are naturally geared towards consolidation and guardianship, but this can be a real opportunity for the family. Second-generation individuals are usually noticeably loyal and conservative and they value relationships, which can be an advantage if directed towards solving the problems of an evolving family office which can no longer be effectively driven forward by one individual.

2. If you are a second-generation individual, are you doing what you want within the family office/businesses or are you there through a sense of duty? If the latter, how can you develop your own goals going forward? Developing a sense of individuality and personal ambition is not bad for the family – it can enhance your energy and commitment.

3. By enhancing your own sense of ownership and value, you can effectively help to develop these skills in your own children, encouraging the third generation's sense of purpose and personal worth.

4. So, being honest, how much ownership and control do you feel you have? If not that much, would you value having more? What do you feel you need to achieve that?

5. As a parent of third-generation children, are you trying to help them develop goals, delay gratification and find a balance between work and play? Are you saying 'no' enough? One of the biggest challenges for second-generation parents is to find the middle ground between setting limits and feeling too restrictive. Have a think about the values you would like your children to have, what you would like them to believe about themselves and the world. Once you have done that, have a think about how to achieve that, in developmental steps. Some ideas for this are also in the next chapter.

Notes and References: Chapter 8

[1]   Berridge, K., et al. (2008) 'Affective Neuroscience of Pleasure: Reward in Humans and Animals'. *Psychopharmacology* 199(3), 457–480. http://www.wireheading.com/pleasure/pleasure.pdf (viewed June 2015).

For general information on the effect of experiences in childhood on the developing brain, see also:

National Scientific Council on the Developing Child. (2005/2014). *Excessive Stress Disrupts the Architecture of the Developing Brain: Working Paper 3.* Updated Edition. Retrieved from www.developingchild.harvard.edu

CHAPTER 9

The Solution – The Third Generation

By the time the wealth cycle reaches the third generation and beyond, the three-generation wealth trap has often been set firmly in motion due to the challenges facing the first and second generations in adapting to their own circumstances. However, this is not inevitable and, with intervention, can be avoided.

At the same time, there are significant challenges facing third-generation individuals and, as with their parents, the second generation, the challenges have become increasingly complex since the original wealth creation phase of the first generation and therefore require a sophisticated set of solutions. The complexity of the issues facing the third generation, both opportunities and challenges, goes a long way to explaining why the three-generation wealth trap appears so difficult to overcome; these are an intricate set of difficulties, requiring a solution which matches them.

What are these challenges, we may ask? What difficulties can third-generation individuals who have grown up with financial security, a multitude of opportunities and, apparently, no limit on their achievement possibly face?

The answer is that the very financial security in which they have grown up, along with the lack of any limits to what is practically possible, changes the entire landscape for a third-generation individual. This chapter considers the personality development, need hierarchy, neurological and psychological impact for post-second-generation individuals and explains why the difficulties they seem to experience so often arise. This chapter also proposes a set of solutions to these issues, with the help of the second generation who, we hope, will understand how to assist with putting in place the right developmental conditions, boundaries and opportunities to enable third-generation individuals to thrive.

Unlike the natural second-generation state of conservation and preservation, or the achievement-driven nature of the first generation, the natural state, without intervention, of a typical third-generation individual is one which is directionless and demotivated without a natural sense of consequence or purpose. This may sound pessimistic and it is not that third generations walk around the world like Eeyore from *Winnie-the-Pooh* – often quite the opposite. But it is often the case that a third-generation individual will struggle to understand the link between actions and consequences and will have an unrealistic (at times over-inflated and at times utterly self-deprecating) sense of their own value and potential to make a meaningful contribution to their families, to their communities and even to their own lives. Where the second generation may have lacked a sense of ownership, what often happens for third-generation individuals is the development of an apparent sense of 'entitlement', but we argue that this comes from a lack of secure self-esteem or of a sense of their own worth as individuals.

It is due to this lack of a sense of consequence, lack of a feeling of purpose and fundamental lack of true self-esteem that addiction and often dangerous risk-taking behaviour is so prevalent amongst third-generation individuals.[1] Because if we have everything that, in theory, we could materially want, we lack the boundaries and sense of value which inhibit the majority of the world's population and prevent some of the excesses of recklessness. And if we do not have a sense of purpose or consequence then how do we learn to put limits on our behaviour? The answer is complicated and yet, when we explain the problem in neurological and psychological terms, in many ways both the causes and the solutions become apparent.

As with the first and second generations, what we don't want to try to do is just make the third generation 'more like' the first or the second, which is what many interventions try to do, with the idea that we can somehow implant a sense of valuing preservation or achievement and all will be well. As we stated before, as well as being essentially impossible due to their life experiences and their neurological and resulting psychological and emotional states (which is why these interventions rarely work), this isn't necessary or desirable, as the solutions which assisted the other generations to meet the challenges they faced are no longer the most appropriate.

What we do want, however, is to enable the third generation to develop a sense of consequence, self-value and purpose, and to help with the growth of reward mechanisms which value commitment, longer-term gratification and living a boundaried existence rather than one free from all limits. Unlike the first and, to an extent, the second generation, in order to thrive, the third generation need to learn how to impose their own personal limitations, not because they 'have to' from an external point of view, but because this will be good for them – and this requires real self-worth and a personal reward structure which values delaying gratification in favour of commitment and task-focused behaviour.

Hopefully, when explained in this way, all the generations can understand that the challenges facing the third generation are significant and inability to find a meaningful place in the world, sometimes demonstrated by addiction, recklessness and an apparent inability to commit to relationships or jobs, or to see any idea through to its conclusion, is purely a sign that the third-generation individual simply has not yet developed the solutions or skills to resolve the challenges they face.[2]

Personality and the Third Generation

Third-generation personalities often come in for a great deal of criticism. They are often, although crucially not always, characterised as lacking direction or motivation, being reckless or arrogant, having a sense of entitlement or lacking an understanding of the world around them. Whilst many of these criticisms are exaggerated to suit the purpose of the person or organisation levelling them, it is often the case that third-generation individuals may seem not to share many of the values or beliefs, the work ethic or the sense of duty or responsibility which characterised their parents' or grandparents' generations.

However, as we have pointed out in this book, we cannot expect third-generation individuals to develop personality structures which are simply enhanced copies or developed versions of their parents' or grandparents', because the circumstances of their lives, their experiences and the subsequent influences on their development – neurologically, psychologically and in terms of their personalities – are totally different.

As we discuss in the section on psychology below, in order for aspects of the brain to develop, we need resistance (like muscle which needs something to push against in order to grow). And so it is with personality in that the lack of 'resistance' in certain areas, and the high levels of resistance in others, are of course likely to lead personalities to develop in certain ways. It is important not to generalise about third-generation individuals and in the introduction to this book we promised to avoid stereotypes. But often the worry for third-generation individuals, and their parents, is how the experience of extreme wealth can be mitigated to ensure that these individuals grow into adults who have a sense of their own value, their own agency and their own potential, rather than lacking motivation and a sense of purpose.

In terms of personality, many (although not all) third-generation individuals develop a preference for activities which are exciting and unpredictable. Myers-Briggs would categorise this as having a strong 'P' or perception focus, pulling towards sensation-based stimulation and lacking concern for societal expectations. Why would this be the case? Well, of course, if a person grows up in a world in which, often from birth, there is a high level of exposure to new sensations (for example, high levels of travel or lots of 'new' things), then the personality will often naturally develop towards an appreciation of the 'new' over that which is more routine or repetitive. And one of the features of life for third-generation individuals is that life is often significantly less routine than that of their peers, whether it is from having multiple homes, living in different countries, changes in staff or personnel around them or having access to experiences which many others do not have due to the limits of resources. This is not the standard, routine and repetitive life of the majority of the population and whilst it offers opportunities for wonderful experiences at an early age, it can bring with it a difficulty in understanding the importance of routine, predictability or the repetitive, which, as we know, characterise much of everyday life at work. Having said that, it can often go the other way, and this is often a feature we see in third-generation individuals: on the one hand a love of the new and of stimulation, but at the same time a level of inflexibility and often a struggle to change course once one has been set.

It is perhaps also unsurprising that third-generation individuals may develop personality structures which are introverted or inwardly-focused, in that their world is often fundamentally different from that of their peers and is not one which is naturally shared except by a very small number of people. Third-generation individuals may grow up feeling separate from general society and culture and may, not unreasonably, learn that the rules which seem to apply for others do not apply for them. This is along with a natural introversion which can mean that they have a tendency to isolate themselves, or to feel isolated or separate from others.

This is not to say that third-generation individuals are not outgoing; they often are, but what can often happen if a person grows up feeling separate from others is that they become naturally inward-focused and learn to 'recharge their batteries' through introversion, as opposed to those who are energised or stimulated by being surrounded by people. What we see as introversion can sometimes be seen, by those criticising third-generation individuals, as a level of arrogance or of narcissism, but we feel this fails to understand the developmental features which underlie the forming of the third-generation individual's personality. And those who criticise perhaps do not fully understand what it is like to grow up surrounded by people, and yet different or separate from them – and the way that this affects personality, which needs to develop certain defences in order to adapt to these circumstances.

The main criticism often levelled at third-generation personalities is that they take unnecessary risks and are reckless. As we point out in the rest of this chapter, to understand risk we need to understand the basic mechanisms of cause and consequence, of risk and reward. Where we are protected against risk or shielded from the consequences of decisions, often through the sufficiency of family resources which can tolerate a certain number of losses, how do we learn consequence and how do we appreciate what risk is?

In fact, it is often a natural parental instinct to protect our children from the consequences of their decisions. I remember once speaking to a friend who was trying to encourage her (young adult but still living at home) son to take more responsibility, including taking charge of putting the bins out once a week, in preparation for him to move into an apartment. Week after week, he failed to put out the bins and she ended up either reminding him or ensuring herself that it was done. When we discussed how she could help him to learn to remember and take responsibility, the only way she could imagine this happening was through there being consequences of forgetting – and by the time he was a young adult, her being mildly cross was insufficient! But when we suggested leaving bin bags in his room, or insisting that he take bags to the local recycling plant in his own time and using his own car when he forgot, she looked at me with a smile – 'Oh, I don't think that would work …' So where is the consequence of our decisions, and how do we learn to take responsibility if there are no consequences? The answer is that we don't.

As this story illustrates, it is not only the families with extreme wealth who struggle to instil a sense of consequence in their children. However, we argue that for wealthy families, it is actually more important that they learn to do so, because the stakes are higher and there are greater opportunities to take risks which are damaging or potentially disastrous.

A note of caution should be applied when using personality profiling, in that such categorisations perhaps undervalue the individual's own experiences and personality – such as Myers-Briggs, which ends, ultimately, in reducing us as humans to sixteen main possibilities without really considering the incredible variation between us all. However, what can be useful in thinking of the main personality 'drivers' for third-generation individuals is thinking about the broad categories as a starting point, using them to consider both potential areas of vulnerability and possible strengths.

If third-generation individuals more often than not tend to show characteristics of the more introverted and sensation-seeking personality types, then this is something which is relevant to how we start to understand the challenges they face, and also gives an indication of the strengths on which we can build. For example, whilst these personality structures may often steer away from routine or predictability, or may be inward-looking and not strongly influenced by societal expectations, there is potential here for real creativity, independence of mind and adaptability – all of which can be immensely positive.

The question of personality types is therefore, as we know, not about 'good' or 'bad', but about how to be mindful of our natural characteristics and work out strategies which enhance our strengths, develop our less natural tendencies and minimise our areas of potential weakness.

Maslow's Hierarchy of Needs

For the third generation, the first two levels of need are a given. There is no lack – indeed there is often a surplus – in the area of physiological need, nor is there (usually) any lack in the area of safety. This allows the individual to achieve a level of fundamental basic security which is different from those of their parents and grandparents and immediately sets them apart. This meeting of need is, of course, what we want for all our children, but for many third-generation individuals, what it means is that there is no struggle against which they can build their psychological 'muscles', their resilience and their sense of 'overcoming' or achievement.

Whereas the first generation are often risk-takers because they have little to lose and everything to gain (and therefore their risk-taking is a calculated course of action based on an unconscious assessment of the potential consequences), many third-generation individuals are risk-takers because they have no sense of consequence or of connection between action and result. Without any insecurity in the areas of need which helped to shape the lives of their grandparents and often, either directly or indirectly, their parents, there is no real sense of what the risk they are taking actually 'is'. It is an abstract risk and is therefore not one which is considered, either consciously or unconsciously, as an action with real potential consequences. Therefore, in some ways, what we might see as a risk is not seen as such by a third-generation individual – because there is no real sense of what failure might feel like.

The third-generation hierarchy of needs effectively 'begins' at the third level, that of belonging, and goes up from there towards self-esteem and self-fulfilment. But without any 'resistance' in the earlier two levels what can happen is that we do not fully value or understand 'belonging', and our self-esteem is built not on our own achievements, but on those of others (which, arguably, is as bad as not having any at all). So the lack often comes for third-generation individuals in the sense of belonging –

'Why do I belong? Where do I belong? With whom do I belong?' – and in self-esteem which is often fragile as a consequence.

In stories from history where there is great hardship and suffering – for example, lack of food, water or shelter – tales of great camaraderie and fellowship stand out. These tales of sharing scant resources or meagre rations are part of the narrative of survival when there is nothing. People have little but they share with others and, in effect, are unconsciously trying to use a 'top-down' approach where a sense of belonging reduces the sense of 'lack' in the areas of safety or physiological need. Of course, as we know, it does not work entirely effectively to eradicate the sense of lack, but it is a natural human tendency to try to 'leapfrog' a level and to see if the benefits which come from a higher level of need can filter down.

So it is the case with third-generation individuals whose self-esteem does not grow organically out of resilience or overcoming challenges presented by lower levels of need. Instead, the tendency is to aim for 'fulfilment' (the top of Maslow's hierarchy) with the idea that 'happiness' will increase self-esteem and will give a more complete sense of belonging. And what third-generation individuals often express is a quest for purpose (or a lack of a sense of the purpose of life). Without a link to the other levels of need, this search for 'fulfilment' is rootless and disconnected. In other words, there is a lack of understanding of the value of things – of material possessions, but also of themselves. A sense of how to assess the real 'value' of the world and their own part within it often does not take root with third-generation individuals. This helps to explain (within the context of Maslow's hierarchy) why many third-generation individuals struggle to find a purpose or 'fulfilment' and instead seem bent on the pursuit of pleasure, without being able to tolerate levels of discomfort or disappointment.

Of course, this is a sketch of a 'third-generation individual' and should be taken as cautiously as the idea of a personality profile. But it does ring true for many and helps us understand the apparent lack, in many third-generation individuals, of the ability to commit to something and work through the process step-by-step, to sacrifice short-term gain for longer-term achievement or to understand how to achieve this holy grail of 'happiness' or 'fulfilment'.

The answer is to provide some opportunities for third-generation individuals to develop resilience, overcome challenges and therefore grow self-esteem naturally. This can be achieved through understanding that some struggle, some resistance, is healthy, and this means that many first- and second-generation parents and grandparents will have to do battle with a natural instinct to provide everything they can, without limits or meaningful restrictions. It is important that, to help the third generation develop this sense of independence and resourcefulness on which their self-esteem can be built, limits are placed on what can be accessed freely. It may feel unkind to set conditions for accessing money when there is plenty – it goes against our natural instinct as parents. But the attitude which first- and second-generation parents and grandparents can helpfully develop is one where we are seeing the long term, not the short term. We are seeing the benefits of learning that we can be self-reliant and develop our own skills, abilities and sense of achievement, and we are passing those on to our children. This is the real transfer of wealth, and it means that we are creating children who are able to tolerate the complexity of the challenges and opportunities that great wealth brings. These children are much less likely to be thrown off by the stallion.

Neurological Development

As we have discussed in previous chapters, our personalities, psychological development and behaviours are directly linked to our neurological development, including the reward pathways in our brains which influence our sense of motivation and personal drivers. Our neurological development also influences the levels of anxiety which we experience in response to different events, and our ability to sustain a positive or stable emotional state.

For third-generation individuals, the 'resistance' which the brain uses to develop different pathways and structures is entirely different from that of the first or second generation. Whereas, for the first generation, there may be significant challenges which require the development of accurate problem-solving abilities and determination to push against limitations experienced during their developmental years (including financial limitations), the third generation will usually have had substantially less opportunity to develop these neurological structures – because there has been less experience of resistance and barriers.

Whereas the second generation may experience challenges which require the development of reward pathways centred around duty, loyalty, regulation and preservation (due in part to growing up in an often fast-changing environment), the third generation do not experience these challenges and instead are required to develop neurological structures which somehow enable them to be motivated, be ambitious and have a sense of purpose without the opposing forces which would make this possible. Just like astronauts lose muscle tone in space due to the lack of gravity, so it is for third-generation individuals who we can criticise for lacking the ability to focus, to consider the consequences of their actions, to find a purpose in life – but without the 'gravitational force' required to do so.

Psychology and Behaviour

As mentioned above, some of the ways in which third-generation individuals are affected are in the areas of 'valuing', both of themselves and of the world around them, and of developing a sense of consequence – or, more specifically, of connecting one set of events with a predicted outcome. Most of us understand that if I spend an amount of money on, say, a new car, I will have that much less money to purchase another item (literally $A - B = C$). But if that consequence does not apply, if I can purchase a new car without any real reduction in the amount I have available for other things, then how would I understand that $A - B = C$? Instead, for me, $A - B = A$. So my sense of basic consequence when it comes to financial matters is incoherent and does not follow certain key processes. Even more so if, when I damage that car, I can simply replace it with another one with no sense of having lost something of significance. And so, in this very simple example, a sense of 'value' and of consequence does not take root.

That instance is related specifically to financial matters, but in terms of personal worth (of ourselves and of others), a similar difficulty in finding value can be a challenge for many third-generation individuals. This is not to do with a lack of praise or due to cold or critical parenting, and is not in any way to suggest that second-generation parents withhold affection or act in such a way to directly damage the self-esteem of their children; often far from it. It is often far more difficult to say 'no', as a second-generation parent, when it is a choice to do so in the genuine interest of the child's emotional and psychological development (which is, to be fair, quite an abstract concept) than it is to say 'no' because we simply can't afford it!

However, in order to develop an accurate sense of self-worth and self-esteem, we need to be able to realistically value ourselves and others, assessing our own strengths and weaknesses. We also need to develop the skills to appropriately tolerate difficult emotions, such as a sense of failure, feelings of disappointment (in ourselves or others) and of sadness, frustration and anger. Accepting our own weaknesses through a process of accurate self-assessment, and tolerating the uncomfortable feelings that may emerge as a consequence of this, is essential to being able to learn how to approach challenges and learn from situations which do not go the way we planned or hoped.

But this is where the real challenge for both the second and the third generation presents itself: how do I, as a second-generation parent, deliberately disappoint my child for a long-term gain, rather than please them for a short-term one? This almost goes against the normal rules of parenting, and we can see from this how the challenges facing second- and third-generation individuals are not the same as for many others. On the basis that second-generation individuals are often very loyal and value relationships highly, to deliberately disappoint a child when it would be possible to say yes and satisfy them (and smooth the relationship in the immediate future rather than create potential conflict or upset) is incredibly difficult.

Considering the above, real self-esteem is therefore not due to an abundance of praise and support but instead comes from learning from our mistakes and, most importantly, learning how to cope with situations which challenge us (along with parental support and encouragement to do so!). Part of the difficulty facing many third-generation individuals is that they are often protected, by the very nature of their world, from the consequences of their mistakes or, where they do acknowledge them, instead of learning how to tolerate the difficult emotions which arise, they learn to distract themselves from situations which provoke emotions which are less than positive.[3] Distraction and diversion activities are therefore often features of third-generation individuals' coping strategies for facing the world, along with a difficulty in tolerating appropriate criticism (either reacting defensively or feeling destroyed by it), which are all signs of a lack of real self-worth.

If we do not learn to tolerate difficult emotions without simply distracting ourselves from them, and do not develop an understanding of our own ability to overcome challenges, then it is perhaps inevitable that we will fail to develop a sense of purpose, of direction or of personal value. We may imagine that we would be a successful restaurateur, actor, hotelier, company director etc., but we do not have the psychological skills to progress through the steps needed or understand the consequences of certain behaviours. Because why would the average third-generation individual understand? They have not gone through the same learning processes that others have and therefore the helpful thing to do is not simply to criticise the end result, as is so often done, but to look at how these skills can be learned.

From these psychological descriptions, it is perhaps easy to see why substance abuse, reckless behaviours, an apparent sense of entitlement and all the other excesses which third-generation individuals may display are so prevalent. But our position is that accurate self-worth and emotional intelligence can be learned and developed and that third-generation individuals are very capable, with the right interventions, of developing the ability to recognise and predict consequences, to limit their own behaviours and to understand their own personal value, and that of the world around them.

Social Structures and Organisational Structures

A third-generation individual's level of psychological development and cognitive functioning will often not be as high as a casual observer might expect. Although presented with many opportunities for learning, much of the experiential learning (or 'learning from experience') for third-generation individuals will have been limited.

As we have said throughout this book, the solving of one layer of problems brings with it a set of challenges which require different and often more complex solutions, and so it is for the world of the third generation and beyond. The world in which the successful third-generation individual exists is inevitably sophisticated in terms of organisational and social structures and needs to be at an advanced level in order to meet the challenges which will be encountered. Whereas, for the first-generation individual, a less complex social and organisational structure was entirely appropriate and met the needs of the individual, their businesses and their family, by the time we approach third generation plus, these types of social or organisational structures will no longer help the family office or the individuals within it to thrive.

As much as anything, we are now, of course, likely dealing with larger numbers of people who are served by the family office, often with diverging ideas or philosophies on life (for example, religious beliefs), on financial management, on philanthropy or on the family versus the individual. One example which recently came to our attention is that of a set of family businesses in the USA where the current CEO (a third-generation individual) has alienated most of his family members to the point where they have now sold their shares in the family business due to concerns over how it is being run. The current CEO is selling assets (equipment, land etc.) to improve the apparent profitability of the company and has made numerous redundancies, including many individuals whose families have worked for the company for several generations. The reason? According to one family member, it is because the current CEO has his eyes on political office and is therefore enhancing the short-term profitability of the company to help fund his political campaign and boost his image as a businessman with a 'dynamic' and financially valuable company portfolio (which the accounts will show).

Whether or not this is actually the case, it is clear from this example that the family members have significantly different ideas as to how the businesses should be run, with some favouring slow growth and strong reliance on solid assets over the alternative promoted by the current CEO. Many of the family members believe that the current CEO is moving the businesses away from their 'roots', which include a strong religious underpinning. More than anything, though, this example shows how relationships, trust and a sense of ownership within the family have broken down with many of the other third-generation individuals simply walking away from the family office, which they no longer trust will be able to meet their needs – and they would rather be out now than liable later.

This brief example shows that by the time the family office reaches the third generation, the organisational and social structures which are needed are far more complex than the more patriarchal structure which usually served the first generation so well. But if, for the reasons previously laid out, the current third generation are limited in terms of their personal psychological and cognitive functioning, how can they help to create (or successfully sustain) family office organisational and social structures which are appropriately sophisticated? So it is no wonder that the third generation often struggle to meet the challenges faced – they have not developed the personal skills and, as a consequence, they will struggle to help the business structures and the organisation of the family office grow to the point where they are able to meet the needs of the third-generation-plus family.

A Template for Third-Generation 'Responsive, Non-Entitlement Trust'

As discussed above, some of the issues for third-generation individuals are difficulties connecting money with value, a lack of a sense of ownership and purpose, and often real struggles with the link between action and consequence.

One way of encouraging appreciation for the opportunities of money, enhancing a sense of personal and social responsibility, and instilling a feeling of ownership and of 'worth' for third generations is to introduce a structured system for access to wealth which is responsive, individualised and aimed at development rather than 'entitlement'.

The question of 'fairness' in families is usually taken to mean that it is a parent's responsibility to ensure each child has the opportunity to meet their potential. So far, so good. However, crucially, this is not equivalent to giving each child exactly the same. That isn't actually 'fair' in a sophisticated sense and actually creates feelings of entitlement and often rivalry between siblings. The same treatment cannot be applied to each child because their needs are different, their personal development will be different and their personalities and psychological structures will be different. For example, if my relatively responsible eleven-year-old son is doing after-school activities and it makes sense for him to have a phone in order that he can keep in contact, does it automatically mean that my nine-year-old son should, by default, have a phone when he turns eleven? Surely that would depend on why he needs it, how sure I am that he will take care of it and how safe he will be with his newly accessed technology. But, of course, many parents give in to the idea that if one child has something at eleven, then it is only 'fair' that the others will too. This is not *true* fairness and instead 'fairness' must take into account a range of factors which are more complex than, for example, a blanket age-related entitlement to certain privileges.

Of course, a phone is a small and specific example (and can relatively easily be withdrawn if the privilege is abused), but what happens when we set up an inheritance structure which is based on an age-related, 'everybody has won, and all must have prizes' (to quote Lewis Carroll) concept of fairness? Should all my children have access to an inheritance simply because they manage to achieve the age of eighteen, twenty-one, twenty-five etc. . . . ?

What we propose is instead a more sophisticated and reciprocal template for a trust where no child has an entitlement to anything. The money which has been created and nurtured by previous generations is there to give them the best opportunities possible to meet their potential. The money should be a springboard to the most amazing life, not the end in itself, nor a burden. The reciprocal arrangement is for responsibility from the recipient. The trust should have a responsiveness to the individual needs of each child, not a 'one size fits all' approach to fairness, and should therefore offer genuine equality, not an arbitrary sort.

As a generic suggestion, one example would be that:

- At twelve, the children are entitled to information about the family businesses and charities.
- At fifteen, they should be able to apply to the trust to get a small amount of money – which is solely distributed to a charity of their choice. They should do some investigation so that they understand the purpose of that charity and what it aims to do.
- At eighteen, they get to apply to the trust for a larger sum of money for a charity, and they get 10% for their own discretionary spending. Their application to the trustees needs to be done by them and it needs to show it meets the policy of the family as already written.
- At twenty-one, they are able to apply for a certain amount of funding to help with their personal developmental process (training, gap year etc.).
- At twenty-five, they can make an application to start their own business, purchase property etc.

The trust structure we have set up here is a developmental and responsive trust because it responds to the needs of each child. The only requirement is that the trust has to decide whether each child must go through each of these stages before they can go on to the next or whether they can, for example, at eighteen, bypass the first two stages and proceed to the opportunity presented to them at that age. As with all issues of management, a clear family mission statement and strong governance are essential because it will be against these that the trustees measure their decisions.

Summary

The responsive trust template above is only a suggestion, but it is one which incorporates strategies for helping with so many of the areas of difficulty for third-generation individuals which we have set out in this chapter. Overall, the aim of any strategy is to help an individual build on their strengths, learn to manage or minimise their weaker areas, and develop a sense of self-worth and of purpose through connection to their families, their communities and beyond. The intention is to help create individuals who are ready for the supercar when they get it, rather than inheriting a set of keys without the skills, abilities or personal development to fully enjoy it safely.

Chapter 9 – A quick reference guide:

1. Third-generation individuals need to develop the skills to realistically value themselves and other people as well as material possessions. Understanding how to assign value is key to success.

2. Third-generation individuals also need to develop an understanding of cause and effect, or 'consequence', which helps with planning of tasks and personal achievement and inhibits reckless or unbounded behaviours.

3. As part of this, third-generation individuals need to be taught 'affect tolerance' or the ability to tolerate, process and learn from difficult emotions without using distraction as the main tool. This 'affect tolerance' enables individuals to overcome challenges, seek to achieve goals and be appropriately self-confident.

4. Part of this tolerance for third-generation individuals is an understanding of delayed gratification or long-term, rather than short-term, gain and satisfaction. For the second-generation parents who raise them, this may mean going against a natural instinct to satisfy and meet their demands.

5. Third-generation individuals, like the family offices and businesses which they may inherit, need to adapt to a complex set of circumstances with a sophisticated set of solutions.

Notes and References: Chapter 9

[1] Berkman, E.T. (2012) 'What is the value of self-control? The intriguing link between self-concept and self-control'. *Psychology Today*, November 5th.

[2] Al'Absi, M. (Ed.) (2007) *Stress and Addiction: Biological and Psychological Mechanisms*. Oxford: Academic Press.

[3] Crews, F., He, J., Hodge, C. (2007) 'Adolescent cortical development: a critical period of vulnerability for addiction'. *Pharmacology, Biochemistry and Behaviour* 86(2), 189–199.

Conclusion

Money is about both opportunity and challenges. The opportunity to have an awesome and exceptional set of life experiences, but the challenge to use it in a way which is enhancing both for ourselves and for future generations.

What any parent wants is for their children to achieve their potential, whatever that potential may be, and what this book has shown are the ways in which we can accept the blessings we have been given, but understand how to build upon them.

As we have set out here, the three-generation wealth trap is often just assumed to be unavoidable, or, where solutions are promised, they look more at the individual aspects of the family office – the financial or organisational structures in place, *or* the relational issues, *or* the individuals. What we hope this book has shown is that it is not enough to look at one aspect alone, but instead what needs to be considered is how all these areas interact and either enhance or degrade the others.

For example, without clear governance it is impossible to put in place the increasingly sophisticated solutions to the problems arising in relation to wealth transfer. But unless the individuals who are to take the family office forward into the next generation have a sense of ownership and a belief in their own ability to be creative and constructive partners in the business of the family office, how can they find these solutions? And if these individuals (often the second generation) lack a sense of ownership or agency (allowing them to effect strong governance), then how can they effectively provide the sense of cause and consequence and instil feelings of purposefulness, value and meaning in their own children? Similarly, for the third generation, if there is no link between value and effort, between risk and reward, no impression of the difference between ownership and entitlement, then how can a person develop the learning (both neurological and psychological) that endeavour is rewarded and that short-term gratification must often take second place to long-term goals?

If it is possible to summarise the personal qualities needed for all generations to succeed and inspire the next generation to do so equally: we need to be flexible, and be compassionate. We need to remember that integrity matters and compatibility matters. Crucially, it isn't healthy to entirely sacrifice your happiness for that of another. We must be able to admit our mistakes, and not to punish other people unnecessarily for theirs. It is essential to make time for people, but, at the same time, to get to a point where we don't need a relationship with others (wanting is different from needing). If we can do this, we will be able to build our own self-esteem and security and have that sense of meaning and the ability to seize opportunity as it presents itself, but always with real self-awareness, understanding and insight. In short, love more and be awesome.

This book has also shown the link between the organisation of the family office or family business governance structures and the stages of development. If we have an increasingly complex situation but a family office which has not evolved to meet this, then this will inevitably lead to decline. At the same time, what we have shown is that the sophistication of the solutions needed for the financial and business structures cannot be considered in isolation and must be developed alongside the growth in skills and abilities of the individuals those structures serve. A third-generation-stage family office, like the individuals it represents, needs to be sufficiently complex and developed to meet the demands which will be placed upon it.

To resolve these issues may sound utopian, but we believe that all of the tools you need to achieve this, you already have at your disposal. The question is how to structure interventions so that they maximise your natural strengths, help you build on the areas you find more difficult and, crucially, ensure that the environment around you (including the structure of the family office) grows and develops with you in order to meet the challenges ahead. With regard to your blessing, grow it, cherish it, use it sensibly. Give yourself good experiences and realise the value in education (of all kinds), and use the money wisely and for both yourself and others.

Lightning Source UK Ltd.
Milton Keynes UK
UKOW02n0659121215

264567UK00001B/10/P